The Waste Land

A Poem of Memory and Desire

TWAYNE'S MASTERWORK STUDIES
ROBERT LECKER, GENERAL EDITOR

The Waste Land,

A Poem of Memory and Desire

NANCY K. GISH

TWAYNE PUBLISHERS • BOSTON

A Division of G.K. Hall & Co.

The Waste Land: A Poem of Memory and Desire
Nancy K. Gish

Twayne's Masterwork Studies No. 13

Copyright 1988 by G.K. Hall & Co.
All rights reserved.
Published by Twayne Publishers
A Division of G.K. Hall & Co.
70 Lincoln Street
Boston, Massachusetts 02111

Typeset in 10/14 Sabon
by Compset, Inc., of Beverly, Massachusetts

Printed on permanent/durable acid-free paper
and bound in the United States of America

Library of Congress Cataloging-in-Publication Data

Gish, Nancy K., 1942–
    The waste land.

    (Twayne's masterwork studies ; no. 13)
    Bibliography: p.
    Includes index.
    1. Eliot, T. S. (Thomas Stearns), 1888–1965.
Waste land. I. Title. II. Series.
PS3509.L43W36485 1988   821'.912   87-31555
ISBN 0-8057-7973-6 (alk. paper)
ISBN 0-8057-8023-8 (pbk. : alk. paper)

Contents

Note on References and Acknowledgments

This book assumes a reader familiar with the text of *The Waste Land*, including the notes, but does not assume knowledge of secondary sources. My aim is to approach the poem in a way that will both clarify its complex structure and meaning and foster appreciation of its poetic values.

I am indebted for many insights to earlier commentators. For the chronology I am especially indebted to Caroline Behr's *T. S. Eliot: A Chronology of His Life and Works* and to Lyndall Gordon's *Eliot's Early Years*.

All quotations from *The Waste Land* are from *The Waste Land: A Facsimile and Transcript of the Original Drafts Including the Annotations of Ezra Pound*, edited by Valerie Eliot. The photograph of Eliot in 1922 is reproduced by the kind permission of the Houghton Library at Harvard University.

I would like to thank Francis McGrath for reading and commenting on parts of the manuscript and Robert Kemp for introducing me to word processing and solving all my computing difficulties.

Chronology:
T. S. Eliot's Life and Works

1888   26 September, T. S. Eliot born in St. Louis, Missouri, youngest of six children (four girls and two boys). His father, Henry Ware Eliot, a successful businessman; his mother, Charlotte Champe Eliot, a former schoolteacher who wrote poetry as well as a life of Eliot's grandfather, William Greenleaf Eliot.

1888–1898   Raised in large family dominated by the Unitarian values of his grandfather. Close relationship with his Catholic nurse, Annie Dunne. The family spends summers on the New England seacoast.

1898–1905   Attends Smith Academy in St. Louis. Puts out his own magazine, the *Fireside*. Poems in the *Smith Academy Record*.

1905–1906   Attends Milton Academy in Milton, near Boston, private preparatory school.

1906   Enters Harvard. Bookish and disciplined student but also enjoys comic strips—"Krazy Kat" and "Mutt and Jeff"—and learns boxing.

1908   Discovers Arthur Symons's *The Symbolist Movement in Literature* (1899), where he encounters the poetry of Jules Laforgue, a major influence on his poetic development. Early poems published in the *Harvard Advocate*.

1909   Receives B.A. Returns in October for M.A. in English literature. Studies with Irving Babbitt and George Santayana, important influences. Begins lifelong friendship with Conrad Aiken.

1910   Receives M.A. Begins writing "Preludes" and "Portrait of a Lady." In October sails to Paris.

1910–1911   Attends Henri-Louis Bergson's lectures at the Sorbonne. Close friendship with Jean Verdenal, who later dies in World War I. Travels to London and Munich. Completes "The Love Song of

J. Alfred Prufrock." Returns to Harvard sporting a malacca cane and hair parted behind.

1912–1913 Studies for Ph.D. in philosophy. Plans dissertation on F. H. Bradley. Continues writing poems.

1914 Bertrand Russell is visiting lecturer at Harvard. Eliot leaves in June for a year at Oxford on a Sheldon Travelling Fellowship. Meets Ezra Pound in London.

1915 World War I breaks out. *Poetry* publishes "The Love Song of J. Alfred Prufrock." Eliot meets and marries Vivienne Haigh-Wood. They share Bertrand Russell's flat. Several early poems published.

1916 Completes doctoral dissertation but never returns to Harvard for degree. Teaches at Highgate Junior School, writes reviews, and lectures on modern poetry.

1917 Begins work for Lloyd's Bank. Rejected by army for health reasons. *Prufrock and Other Observations* published by the Egoist Press.

1918–1919 *Ezra Pound: His Metric and Poetry* published by Knopf. Publishes reviews and articles, including the first part of "Tradition and the Individual Talent." Eliot's father dies, 8 January 1919.

1920 *Ara Vos Prec* published by Ovid Press. *The Sacred Wood*, published by Methuen, establishes Eliot as a serious critic.

1921 Vivienne, always in poor health, breaks down and convalesces in the country. Eliot's mother, sister, and brother visit from the United States. Eliot sees Stravinsky's *Le Sacré du Printemps*, writes essays on Marvell, Dryden, and the Metaphysical poets, and reads in *Ulysses*. He is also writing early sections of *The Waste Land*. In September Eliot's health gives way, and he is granted a three-month leave from Lloyd's Bank. Convalescing in Margate and Lausanne, Eliot completes the original version of *The Waste Land*, which he shows to Ezra Pound. Together they cut more than half its length and make many revisions.

1922 *The Waste Land* is published in the *Dial* and receives the *Dial's* annual award of $2,000. Eliot sends John Quinn the original manuscript as evidence of Pound's contribution. The manuscript is mislaid and lost until 1968. *The Waste Land* appears in England also in the first edition of the *Criterion*, edited by Eliot. Boni & Liveright publish the poem in book form, adding the notes that appear in all subsequent editions.

1924 John Quinn dies. *Homage to John Dryden: Three Essays on*

Poetry of the Seventeenth Century increases Eliot's recognition as an important critic.

1925   "The Hollow Men" published in the *Dial*. Eliot leaves Lloyd's Bank to become a director of Faber & Gwyer. Wears a bowler hat, black coat, and striped trousers. *Poems 1909–1925* published by Faber & Gwyer.

1927   Joins the Church of England and becomes a naturalized British citizen. Faber & Gwyer publish "The Journey of the Magi," the first of Eliot's four "Ariel Poems." His poetry and prose become increasingly focused on religious themes.

1928   "A Song for Simeon" published by Faber & Gwyer. In *For Lancelot Andrewes* Eliot announces that his position is "classicist in literature, royalist in politics, and Anglo-Catholic in religion."

1929   "Animula" published by Faber & Faber.

1930   Gives six radio talks on seventeenth-century writers. "Ash-Wednesday" published by Faber & Faber. "Marina," the final "Ariel Poem," published by Blackamore Press. Marriage with Vivienne, always plagued with difficulties, becomes increasingly strained.

1932   Travels to United States to give Charles Eliot Norton Lectures at Harvard. *Selected Essays 1917–1932* published by Faber & Faber.

1933   Separates from Vivienne. Returns to United States to give Page-Barbour Lectures at the University of Virginia. Charles Eliot Norton Lectures published as *The Use of Poetry and the Use of Criticism*.

1934   Page-Barbour Lectures published as *After Strange Gods*. Eliot's career as a playwright begins with *Sweeney Agonistes*— a haunting murder story recited in jazz rhythm—and *The Rock*—a religious pageant play.

1935   Writes *Murder in the Cathedral*. First performance in the Chapter House of Canterbury Cathedral to critical acclaim.

1936   *Essays Ancient and Modern* published by Faber & Faber. *Collected Poems 1909–1935* includes "Burnt Norton," the first of the *Four Quartets*.

1939   Last issue of the *Criterion*. Publishes *The Idea of a Christian Society*. Increasingly writes on need for Christian values. *The Family Reunion* opens at the Westminster Theatre. On 3 September Britain declares war on Germany. Because of the bombing, Eliot moves to Surrey, where he writes "East Coker."

Old Possum's Book of Practical Cats published by Faber & Faber.

1940–1944   During the bombing of London, Eliot serves as a fire watcher on the roof of Faber & Faber. Continues to lecture and write on religious themes. "East Coker," "The Dry Salvages," and "Little Gidding" published successively in *New English Weekly*.

1945   Travels to Paris after war to visit old friends, bringing soap and China tea. Ezra Pound arrested for pro-Fascist broadcasting in Rome. Eliot requests public support from poets to stand by Pound.

1946   Takes a room in John Hayward's flat in London. Writes in praise of Pound.

1947   Vivienne Eliot dies in a nursing home.

1948   Receives the Order of Merit from George VI. Receives the Nobel Prize for literature. *Notes towards the Definition of Culture* published by Faber & Faber. Eliot dines with the king and queen and has a private audience with the pope.

1949   *The Cocktail Party* opens at the Edinburgh Festival. Accompanies Arnold Toynbee on a six-week tour of Germany, lecturing on problems of European unity.

1952   *The Complete Poems and Plays 1909–1950* published by Faber & Faber.

1953   *The Confidential Clerk* opens at the Edinburgh Festival. Over 2,500 people attend Eliot's lecture, "The Three Voices of Poetry," later published by Cambridge University Press.

1955   Receives the Hanseatic Goethe Award in Hamburg.

1956   Delivers lecture on "The Frontiers of Criticism" at the University of Minnesota and describes his own notes to *The Waste Land* as a "remarkable exposition of bogus scholarship."

1957   Marries Valerie Fletcher, his secretary. His second marriage is to be very happy. *On Poetry and Poets* published by Faber & Faber.

1958   *The Elder Statesman,* dedicated to his wife, produced at Edinburgh Festival. Ezra Pound released.

1959   Receives the Dante Gold Medal in Florence. Pope John XXIII commends Eliot for services to the Christian faith.

1962   *Collected Plays* published by Faber & Faber.

1963   *Collected Poems 1909–1962* published by Faber & Faber.

1964   Eliot's dissertation, *Knowledge and Experience in the Philos-*

ophy of F. H. Bradley, published by Glasgow University Press. Eliot remarks, "I do not pretend to understand it." Groucho Marx visits Eliot; they share fondness for cats, cigars, and puns.

1965   Eliot dies, 4 January, at home in London. The *Times* obituary calls him "the most influential English poet of his time."

1967   Memorial stone for Eliot placed in Westminster Abbey.

1971   The rediscovered original manuscript of *The Waste Land*, edited by Valerie Eliot, published by Faber & Faber.

T. S. ELIOT
*By permission of the Houghton Library,
Harvard University*

1

Historical Context

T. S. Eliot was born in 1888, just two years before the last great Indian battle at Wounded Knee and five years after the completion of three transcontinental railroad lines. The American frontier, according to a census report, had ended by about 1890. When Eliot died, in 1965, the nuclear age was already twenty years old, travel was by intercontinental jet, and the new frontier was space. Nothing has been more characteristic of the modern age than extreme and rapid change, and Eliot's life spanned most of that time. Modern artists and writers have felt themselves to be facing a new world of increasing complexity and difficulty for which new modes of poetry, painting, and music must be found. For his contemporaries, Eliot seemed to articulate the modern world, to evoke its characteristic visions and moods.

St. Louis, Missouri, where Eliot was born and grew up, was still on the western edge of settled territory in the late nineteenth century. When his father, Henry Ware Eliot, was a boy, Indian camps lay just outside the town. By the time of Tom's childhood, St. Louis had become a principal manufacturing city, and his father had become a wealthy businessman. It was a pattern common in the nation: the movement of population to cities, the rise of business, and the concentration of wealth. For Tom it meant growing up in a comfortable and educated family who assumed he would go to college and rise in the world.

But like other cities, St. Louis presented stark contrasts of rich and poor. Both there and in Boston, when Eliot attended Harvard, the poor lived in slums, sad streets of cheap smells and blowing paper and shabby hotels to be chronicled in his early poems. In the growing cities as in the entire country, waves of immigrants filled these slums, dividing the population between groups of foreign-born poor who worked in factories and the older native-born who had succeeded in business and who often felt, as did Eliot's family, a strong commitment to duty, education, social concern, and hard work. Indeed, Eliot himself was to become a successful publisher with a character for restraint, hard work, and public involvement.

During his youth, in the 1880s and 1890s, Americans experienced social unrest and depression as well as industrial development at home and the rise of America as a world power. With the Spanish-American War (1898) and the acquisition of possessions in the Pacific, including the Philippines, America made a major shift in policy from isolationism to involvement with other world powers.

While Eliot grew up amid this massive social and political change, he was also being educated in a world of ideas and European intellectual development. In fact, his reported interests and the memories he has written down were largely about poetry and philosophy. He went to a Harvard that had become a center of scholarship and knowledge, and looked to French models for his poetry. Yet he used the techniques of French symbolist writers to depict alienated figures, American and upper-class, wandering the lonely and empty back streets of American city slums.

If turn-of-the-century America provided the context for Eliot's youth and early poems, his adult life was lived in an England successively engulfed in world war and engaged in major economic reform. In the last decades of the nineteenth and first decade of the twentieth century, England experienced many patterns similar to those in America: the move to the cities, increasing division between wealth and poverty, social tension and labor unrest, demands for women's rights, and, for many, a pervading sense of radical change. Yet the Edwardian period (1901–1910) seemed—for the middle and upper classes—to be a time of security and happiness, a series of golden summers and garden parties, frequent mail service and easy travel with no need for passports. "The Great War" changed the world. After World War I, the English people felt separated from that old life by what Winston Churchill called "a measureless gulf."

In August 1914 Eliot and the war, as Wyndham Lewis recalled, arrived in England together. Although Eliot tried to enlist, he was rejected for health reasons and never served; the war was not a direct experience for him. What he did experience was the effect of large-scale mobilization and wholesale slaughter on the civilian population at home and later the division of feeling between those who fought and those who stayed at home.

When it was over in 1918, three quarters of a million British soldiers had died, enormous resources had been spent, a brief economic boom gave way in 1920 to rising unemployment, soldiers and civilians felt estranged, and—perhaps most important—old values and beliefs were no longer secure. Women cut their hair and shortened their skirts. Manners and morals were looser. Young people danced all night to jazz and ragtime music. Life seemed uprooted and uncertain, and a mood of deep disillusion set in along with a rejection of old certainties and constraints. Whether good or bad, the world was different, and art changed with it.

In one sense, Eliot's poetry appears disconnected from the political and social upheavals of both America and England in his time. He seldom writes directly of immediate events, and he tends to explore an inner world of unease and anxiety projected onto contemporary urban landscapes rather than political or social events. The latter appear, when they do, primarily as image or characterization. We know, for example, that Miss Nancy Ellicott smokes and dances all the modern dances, that the typist is a single working woman, that Lil's husband has just come back from the war. But the great events of his time are seldom directly addressed in the poems.

In another sense, however, Eliot's work derives immediately from the social context in which he lived. Like other modern artists and unlike his immediate predecessors, he chooses cities as his settings and contrasts the wealthy and the poor who live there. His early characters walk through the sleazy streets of American slums and note their poignant life. New technology appears without concern for traditional poetic beauty. Taxis throb in his streets. Gramophones play jazz records. Cigarette ends and sandwich papers float on the Thames. Smoke and cocktail smells fill the bars. And even the early poems express a modern malaise. "The Love Song of J. Alfred Prufrock," when it was published in 1917, seemed escapist to some in its disconnection from the overwhelming experience of war, but to others it expressed the modern temperament. When *The Waste Land* appeared in 1922, it was quickly felt to articulate a profound sense of the sterility, fragmentation, and disillusion of its time.

While the scenes, characters, and moods of Eliot's poems reflect the history of his time, his poetry is "modern" in other important ways that reflect changing literary and poetic technique. In his search for poetic models he had looked to the French symbolist poets. Influenced especially by Jules Laforgue, he developed a poetry that was ironic, conversational, and lacking in narrative sequence. He was influenced also by other intellectual developments, especially Sir James Frazer's study of ancient religions, *The Golden Bough*, which provided images of cyclic renewal for *The Waste Land*, and James Joyce's use of myth as a kind of underlying structure for seemingly disordered material. His classical and philosophical studies provided a rich source of allusion and reference for newly complex and intellectual poetry.

The year 1922 marked the publication of both Joyce's *Ulysses* and Eliot's *The Waste Land*. Along with the music of Stravinsky, the paintings of Wyndham Lewis, and early cinema, they signaled a new kind of art that would express life in the twentieth century. A generation of poets and critics came to see Eliot as the intellectual spokesman for their time. He remained, throughout his life, respected and acknowledged as one of the most important poets of his age, even when poetry began to shift in other directions.

The late 1920s and 1930s were a time of depression and anxiety in England. The rise of Hitler in Germany and the Spanish Civil War caused continuing unease. In 1939 England and Germany were again at war. During these years Eliot became steadily more involved in religious questions. In 1927 he joined the Church of England. His poetry, too, changed from depicting the despair of modern life to portraying a difficult personal journey toward faith. While many readers found his new style a betrayal of his early stark vision, others found in it a valid and moving response to the modern dilemma, a return to belief in the face of horror. During World War II he served as a fire watcher in London, an experience described in "Little Gidding," the last of the *Four Quartets*. Like *The Waste Land, Four Quartets* is a response to the disruption and anguish of war; unlike the earlier poem, it offers a kind of faith and promise as definitely attainable. In style the later work is more meditative and abstract, and more pointed toward a specific commitment to belief.

In his later years Eliot turned primarily to writing plays. He turned also to writing cultural and social criticism focused on the need for a society organized as a Christian community. From the despair of his early work in the face of a radically changing and disturbing world, he moved throughout his life toward a return to conservative values held in the face of apparent loss. His response represents one strategy for coping with the ongoing and rapid shifts of modern life. His readers have tended to prefer either the early or the late poetry, depending on whether they find that return to traditional faith possible.

2

The Importance of the Work

The question of literary value is complex. We must distinguish, first of all, between the importance of literature in our lives and the importance of any specific text. Literature defines and creates our world. In poems, plays, novels, and stories we imagine and recognize our world and ourselves. In Othello we see our own capacity for irrational anger, or, perhaps more accurately, in reading *Othello* we discover that anger in ourselves. In *The Mill on the Floss* we recognize the network of constraints and limits within which all women live their lives. Literature is essential because it constantly re-creates and extends our understanding of humanity.

We do not, however, treat all literature as equally important. Some works have seemed to speak more profoundly or movingly than others, and some have sustained the interest of generation after generation. This has been true of *The Waste Land*. Many have considered Eliot to be the most important poet of his time, and although this judgment has also been questioned, his poetry continues to be read, studied, and admired. To evoke and sustain such a response, a work of art must be both aesthetically and intellectually satisfying. That is, it must be both a source of pleasure and a way of knowing the world.

The Importance of the Work

In its vivid imagery, musical virtuosity, and complexity of form, *The Waste Land* has been found by most readers to be aesthetically satisfying at a very deep level. Moreover, in its own time it seemed highly original and technically innovative. While we have become accustomed to such poetic techniques as allusion, ironic juxtaposition, and sudden shifts in imagery and style, Eliot's use of them seemed strikingly new in 1922; they added to a complexity of idea the complexity of an unfamiliar style. The effect of these techniques has retained its value. Reading the poem carefully, one is rewarded by unexpectedly rich associations. In the opening passage, for example, the summer shower of rain is more poignant for its link to the disturbing rain of April. And the wet hair of the hyacinth girl picks up the memory of spring rain again to associate her anticipation of love with the yearly resurgence of life and growth.

Eliot's poetic mastery goes beyond imagery. He has a fine ear for rhythm and musical effect and an ability to produce many moods and tones. He ranges from the lyric beauty of "Inexplicable splendour of Ionian white and gold" to the jazz rhythm of "O O O O that Shakespeherian Rag—" to the crude conversational style of Lil's friend, "And if you don't give it him, there's others will, I said." Eliot's skill at both metric variation and precise, intense images is maintained in passage after passage.

The rhythms and images of *The Waste Land* draw in and absorb the reader. But the poem would not be so important if its excellence were technical only. Its immediate and sustained value rests on the manner in which poetic skill reveals a way of thinking and feeling about the world. The poem addresses itself to fundamental issues of life and death and to human longing for meaning and value. In the years between the wars its fusing of loss and desire seemed to capture the essence of modern experience. But because Eliot grounded that sense of loss and desire in ancient myths, the poem seemed also to express a permanent human condition and thus to have a broad and continuing appeal. The psychological and spiritual experience presented in *The Waste Land* may be read as a vision of the human condition, disconnected from permanent values or divine purpose or human love, and a longing for a renewal of life. Or it may be read as a personal and acute anguish in the face of one's deepest fears about death, loss, and betrayal. But it has consistently been able to evoke an intense sense of what it means to be mortal, limited, conscious of failure, and yet yearning toward some inexpressible possibility.

Because *The Waste Land* so effectively defined what many readers in the 1920s recognized as their own condition, it was very quickly discussed and appreciated by critics and writers. And because it was admired by those who looked for new ways to express modern experience, it was seen to justify radically changed styles and themes. Younger poets were influenced by it to write in similar ways, and critics took it as a model for judging other work. It became important both for its expression of the mood of its time and for the great impact it had on subsequent poetic techniques and values. To a large extent, what is called "Modern" is what resembles *The Waste Land* in theme and style.

Because it has had so profound an impact on its readers and on subsequent poetry, *The Waste Land* must clearly be seen as historically important. But its value for us depends on the response of readers who bring to it changing expectations. One way of judging that is to ask whether we can continue to find pleasure in its imagery and music and whether we can continue to find in it fresh and interesting ways of understanding human experience. Although poetry is written differently today, readers still respond to Eliot's rhythmical control and intricacy of form. His complexity and variety allow for a constant freshness and sense of discovery. Moreover, the experience and meaning of the poem are neither simple nor final. Recent interpretations have shifted emphasis from the structures of myth that seem to underlie the poem to the deeply personal emotion it reveals. Like Shakespeare's plays or George Eliot's novels, it has come to mean new things to new readers. Its continuing importance depends on its capacity to provoke new readings and uncover new ways of knowing the world. Each reader is involved in integrating its historic and personal value.

3

Critical Reception

Unlike many writers whose work only slowly came to be recognized, T. S. Eliot achieved an early and lasting fame. Many of his contemporaries, including William Carlos Williams, H. D., and even to some extent Ezra Pound, have become increasingly appreciated as we have learned to read their work, and we are only beginning to recognize the greatness of others, such as the Scottish poet Hugh MacDiarmid, but writers and critics almost immediately took up the study and praise of *The Waste Land*. By the 1930s it had become the object of serious academic attention, and it has been canonized in anthologies and university courses. Eliot himself was quoted, honored, and granted awards for his contributions to literature. *The Waste Land* continues to be taught in almost all survey courses in poetry as well as courses in modern literature, and Eliot remains a central figure in modern poetry.

The initial reviews of *The Waste Land,* however, were mixed. Some were extremely negative. The controversy it has subsequently engendered was thus present from the beginning. But whether praising or denigrating, critics have consistently paid attention to the poem and agreed that, for good or ill, it is important. The reviews of 1922 and

1923 set both the tone and the terms of the debate. On the negative side, it was called a "mad medley," an "unhappy composition," and "so much waste paper." The style was described as full of "blatancies" and parody without taste or skill. The notes were seen as a substitute for poetry and the quotations as a substitute for originality. F. L. Lucas, reviewing the poem for the *New Statesman*, summed it up: "All this is very difficult; as Dr. Johnson said under similar circumstances, 'I wish it were impossible.'" But strong influences were also brought to bear to claim *The Waste Land* as a major success. The editors of the *Dial*, which first published the poem in America in November 1922, were committed to promoting it. They gave Eliot the *Dial's* annual award of two thousand dollars, and Gilbert Seldes, the managing editor, both commissioned a review by Edmund Wilson and reviewed it himself in the *Nation*. Seldes, praising the poem for both its poetic skill and its content, linked it with Joyce's *Ulysses* as a work that had "expressed something of supreme relevance to our present life in the everlasting terms of art." Rejecting complaints about its supposed formlessness, he claimed that a closer look revealed both its hidden form and the necessity of that form for the specific emotion evoked. The review he commissioned from Wilson appeared in the *Dial* in December 1922 and was later incorporated into Wilson's influential book *Axel's Castle*. It praised Eliot's work as having brought a new personal rhythm into the language and having expressed the experience and mood of the postwar world.

Other voices joined in praise of the new poem. Ezra Pound called it a masterpiece, "one of the most important 19 pages in English." Conrad Aiken wrote a long, mainly favorable review in the *New Republic* in 1923, calling it "one of the most moving and original poems of our time" despite what he considered its lack of coherence or unity. It succeeded, he said, "by virtue of its incoherence, not of its plan." In 1928 E. M. Forster said that Eliot was the poet of a whole generation. Subsequent readers and critics have accepted that judgment, and with few exceptions, the early supporters were acknowledged to have recognized a major work of our time.

While the positive assessment of *The Waste Land* prevailed, the arguments over its meaning, coherence, and poetic form continued. The early reviews, good and bad, opened a debate that continues to-day. Among the many positions put forward, several key issues emerged that remained the focus of later criticism. Perhaps the most immediate and important was the validity and function of Eliot's notes and quotations. Those who disliked the poem found the erudition distracting or confusing if not pedantic and unpoetic. Those who liked it justified the sources and allusions as the very basis of a new and significant poetic technique. A second, and related, issue was the problem of form. Did the poem have any unity or progression, and if so, what was it? Even Conrad Aiken, who admired it, denied that it was coherent. Edmund Wilson, on the other hand, considered it a complete expression of the theme of emotional starvation and insisted that Eliot was able to bring all his various sources into a coherent relation. A third focus of discussion was the central concern of the poem as a personal quest or a social and cultural critique. Was its primary theme individual or social? For Aiken it invited us into a mind, a consciousness; for C. Day Lewis it was "chiefly important as a social document." A fourth issue, which was perhaps most hotly debated initially and has recurred intermittently since, is the poetic skill and effect of individual passages as well as the whole. The accusation that it was filled with parody, "blatancies," and clumsily inserted quotation was countered with claims of musical organization, irresistible rhythms, and mastery of "difficult transitions" and "delicate collocations." Taken together, these four concerns with the quotations and notes, the unity or progression, the individual or social focus, and the poetic quality can be found in one form or another as key threads in nearly all critical commentary on *The Waste Land*.

One of the most important early commentaries was written by I. A. Richards. In 1926 he included a discussion of *The Waste Land* in a book entitled *Principles of Literary Criticism*. In it he raised each of the four key issues and in each case found a positive value in Eliot's method. He defended the use of allusion and quotation as a technical device for compression and made a virtue of the lack of any coherent intellectual thread. The items in the poem, he claimed, are united "by

11

the accord, contrast, and interaction of their emotional effects." What they ultimately express is the "plight of a whole generation," and they do so with the stamp of originality. "Only those unfortunate persons who are incapable of reading poetry," said Richards, "can resist Mr. Eliot's rhythms."[1]

In the 1930s three critics defined what became for several decades the dominant interpretation of the poem. They accepted Richards's ideas that the allusion and quotation worked to compress many complex feelings and ideas into vivid, intense images and that the poem was broadly social in its theme, and they shared Richards's admiration of the poetry, but they assumed a need for unity in any work of art, and they argued that *The Waste Land* was, in fact, carefully unified. The commentaries of F. R. Leavis, F. O. Matthiessen, and Cleanth Brooks became classics, from which much later criticism derived.

Leavis acknowledged what he called the "rich disorganization of the poem," but he took as a point of departure Eliot's notes on Tiresias in claiming a fundamental unity as well. It had, according to Leavis, the unity of an inclusive consciousness represented by Tiresias. The seeming disjointedness he saw as an expression of the present state of civilization in which traditions and cultures mix, but the anthropological background evoked a sense of the unity of life. Thus what Leavis did was apply Eliot's own critical doctrines of impersonality and mythic structure to help explain the poem, specifically using Eliot's claim that Tiresias combines all the figures in the poem and joins past and present, male and female, as well as the notion that unity derives from the use of myth.

The use of Eliot's own criticism to explain his work was carried much further by F. O. Matthiessen. In *The Achievement of T. S. Eliot* Matthiessen moved back and forth between the criticism and the poetry, demonstrating how one could be used to understand the other. In examining *The Waste Land* he drew on Eliot's notes to argue that the overall structure of the poem was in fact based on the fertility rituals and Grail legends described in Jessie Weston's *From Ritual to Romance*. Using Eliot's analysis of James Joyce's *Ulysses*, Matthiessen applied the same method to *The Waste Land*. Eliot had said that Joyce used myth to give order and form to the formlessness of modern experience, and Matthiessen argued that Eliot found in Weston the same function. She provided a "scaffold" for the poem, a principle of unity on which all the many disparate kinds of material could be hung. Matthiessen thus added to Leavis's claim of a unity of consciousness the claim of a unity of content, that is, a background story to which all the references could be linked. For Matthiessen the allusions were not separable and disconnected but part of a system of ideas.

Cleanth Brooks carried the suggestions of Leavis and Matthiessen to a fully developed and detailed interpretation of the poem as a complex but carefully structured whole. He acknowledged that the study of a system of symbols might be merely the scaffolding of the poem but regarded a scaffolding as essential for understanding. His analysis focused on the theme, which he defined as the contrast of two kinds of life and two kinds of death: "Life devoid of meaning is death; sacrifice, even the sacrificial death, may be lifegiving, an awakening to life." Brooks demonstrated the working out of this theme in a section-by-section analysis of the poem, focusing on the sources and quotations as a set of interrelated symbols dominated by the fertility ritual/ Grail legend story described in Weston.

Although Leavis, Matthiessen, and Brooks differed on details, they agreed on several fundamental points. All considered *The Waste Land* to be a unified work of art in which the allusions and quotations formed a fundamental structural principle. They accepted Eliot's doctrine of the impersonality of poetry and defined the poem as a cultural or social critique in which personal experience, if present at all, was made universal and symbolic of modern consciousness. And they agreed on its poetic excellence and importance. These positions, in various forms, remained dominant in Eliot criticism for the next three decades and are influential still. Disagreement, sometimes harsh, was occasionally voiced. Ivor Winters in 1943, and Karl Shapiro and Graham Hough in 1960, for example, denied that the poem had either unity or great skill, but they accepted the terms of debate already set in arguing that unity was the issue. For the most part, critics continued to elaborate on and refine the prevailing ideas.

During the 1940s and 1950s the number of books and articles on Eliot continued to increase. Several key studies developed specific and detailed ways of reading *The Waste Land*. Discussion continued to focus on the issues already defined, but new readings approached them from different directions. Elizabeth Drew based her analysis of unity in Jungian psychology. Grover Smith wrote an extremely detailed and exhaustive study of the use of sources, carrying the method of Cleanth Brooks to its furthest limit. Emphasis was sometimes given to the personal experience in the poem, but those who considered it from this perspective did not exclude the significance of the mythic material. Kristian Smidt, in *Poetry and Belief in the Work of T. S. Eliot,* rejected the notion that the poem expressed the "disillusionment of a generation" and saw it instead as a personal dilemma expressing a general modern predicament, the loss of faith in an absolute. In *A Reader's Guide to T. S. Eliot* George Williamson noted that Eliot finds in individual experience a permanent human experience and attended more to the subtleties of emotion in the poem. But although he acknowledged that his interpretation might "minimize the anthropological framework," he also denied that the poem could be adequately understood independently of that framework. In addition to studies of the poem as a whole, much scholarship was devoted to tracking down sources not given in the notes, such as the identity of Marie or the words to an actual song called "That Shakespearian Rag." The intricacies of individual images and the primary effect of individual sections were analyzed in detail.

But despite the extent and increasing sophistication of explication, the poem resisted final explanations. Within the broad range of agreement, debates arose, perhaps most notably on the degree of progression exhibited in the poem and the nature of the conclusion. For some readers, the Grail story provided a narrative that could be traced in the sequence of Eliot's scenes. For others, it provided only a broad concept of fundamental human experience on which *The Waste Land* could draw for comparison, contrast, and resonance. Thus for Grover Smith the Grail quest could be traced through the poem with only slight variations, while for Williamson and Drew the poem showed no progression despite its overall unity of theme. In like manner, critics who agreed on the idea that the poem portrayed a quest for salvation disagreed on whether the conclusion revealed an answer. Was the poem a rejection of belief and a statement of despair or a longing for renewed faith ending in the renewal of the land and the coming of rain?

While the questions of unity, erudition, personal or social focus, and quality have continued to concern critics—F. C. McGrath's systematic study of the use of Weston appeared in 1976, for example—new interests also began to emerge in the 1960s along with some stronger objections to the traditional readings. Along with Graham Hough and Karl Shapiro, other critics questioned the general assumptions about the poem and the general approval of its style. David Craig called it defeatist; C. K. Stead objected to substituting the sources and notes for the poem; and many critics, such as Frank Kermode, called for new ways of reading it.

Perhaps the most interesting new development, however, was an increasing interest in the composition and publishing history of the text. One major modern scholar, Hugh Kenner, was interested very early in the details of the poem's creation. In *The Invisible Poet* (1959) he pieced together much of the then available information and recognized that the poem had not been written as a single consecutive work but was cut from a longer, loosely linked group of poems. He speculated that the original had constituted a larger whole and that the note about Tiresias was an attempt to supply the poem with "a nameable point of view." Another scholar, Daniel H. Woodward, tracked down more information, and in 1964 wrote an article entitled "Notes on the Publishing History and Text of *The Waste Land*." These studies increased interest in the relation between what was now known to be an altered text and whatever original had preceded it.

In 1968 the original manuscript of *The Waste Land* was discovered, and in 1971 a facsimile edition was published. The original version was discovered to be not only much longer but in many ways quite different from the published text. With this discovery, interest in the poem was strongly renewed and pointed in different directions. It no longer seemed possible to account for the poem as a unified whole organized in patterns suggested by Jessie Weston's book. Nor did the standard explanations of theme and symbolism seem to illuminate the original or the nature of the changes. Two collections of essays on the poem illustrated new directions for commentary: *The Waste Land in Different Voices,* edited by A. D. Moody (1974), and *Eliot in His Time,* edited by A. Walton Litz (1973). Both are concerned with new ways of thinking about the poem in light of discoveries about its composition. The essays in Moody's collection focus on Eliot's use of other sources besides Weston and on his links with music and modern painting. Those in Litz's edition emphasize the text itself, the history of its composition, and the significance of the original form and Eliot's alterations.

Much of the interest in Eliot in the 1970s was also directed toward biography. Eliot's own criticism had denied the value of biography in interpretation of poetry, and for the most part critics had accepted that view in reading his work. But as memoirs began to appear after his death, the relation of his life and work came to seem increasingly important. A series of biographical books appeared, initially focused on personal memories. Later Lyndall Gordon, in *Eliot's Early Years,* brought together important biographical information with a study of the early poetry. The most recent of these books, *T. S. Eliot: A Life* (1984) by Peter Ackroyd, is a full-length, detailed biography.

The combination of biographical information and studies of the text's creation have led to fresh ways of thinking about *The Waste Land* as a more personal, immediate, and fragmented work than the traditional readings acknowledged. At the same time, the presence in the text of references to a unifying myth have had to be taken into account. The result has been a reopening of questions once treated as settled and a consequent openness to a wide range of approaches. Moreover, current scholarship tends to be skeptical about assumptions of unity and coherent meaning in any text. The very richness and complexity of language, its range of connotation and reference, mean that any text evokes a variety of readings. With a text so intricate and layered as *The Waste Land,* there seems no possibility of a discoverable authoritative reading that can be called its "meaning."

One critic defined the issue by suggesting that the poem is itself about the credibility of language and by analyzing the kinds of language it employs, such as quotation, popular speech, the speech of speakers, prophetic speech, and possible supernatural speech.[2] Others have discussed the system of allusion as a relation between reader and author, the relation between the text and the notes as different forms of thinking, the forms of language as a way of pointing to language itself rather than an outside meaning, or the significance of silence, as in the lost words and the speech of nonhuman agents like the nightingale or the thrush.[3]

Like the interest in biography or textual composition, the attention to language itself opens up *The Waste Land* to insights and perceptions that go beyond a particular interpretation and reflect on the place of poetry in human life, both Eliot's and his readers'. We now know, for example, that his personal and psychological condition at the time of writing helped condition the form of the poem. At the same time, the poem as it stands may suggest the ways in which all language functions.

In tracing the critical reception of *The Waste Land* I have concentrated on the academic approaches brought to bear on it and the ways in which scholars and poets have evaluated it because the very difficulty of the poem has largely determined its major audience. Eliot once said that he would like to write for an uneducated audience, but his readers have mainly been the educated. Whole generations of university students have read, studied, and been moved by the poem, which continues to be anthologized and taught as a central modernist work. While the difficulty that may have defined its audience has been deplored by some as separating art from the general population, it has also been defended as a way of creatively altering our thinking and feeling. What is more important, perhaps, is that the richness and possibility contained in that complexity allow for continuing reexamination and rethinking. By outliving the many formulas developed to explain it, *The Waste Land* testifies to the vital and fascinating relation between art and human understanding.

A READING

4

Sources and Composition:
The Creation of the Text

The first readers of *The Waste Land* were puzzled, fascinated, sometimes deeply impressed, sometimes annoyed. Initial readings of the poem are still liable to produce strong and possibly mixed responses. Drawn in at once by the compelling rhythms and images of the opening lines, the reader is suddenly dropped into Marie's mundane and unexplained conversation and as inexplicably shifted to an anguished cry in a stony desert. No sooner are we caught by the heady scent of hyacinths and the poignance of failed desire than Madame Sosostris arbitrarily appears to display her knowledge of fortune-telling. Scenes, styles, rhythms, moods shift and change without warning or recognizable connection. To early readers, expecting straightforward narrative or logical continuity, this was either meaningless or startlingly fresh and original. To us it is likely to seem deceptively familiar but no less complex or confusing.

Although we have become accustomed to modern poetry without obvious sequence or traditional forms, *The Waste Land* remains difficult and enigmatic. Not only is it fragmented in ways that continue to elude simple or consistent interpretation, but it seems to demand a knowledge of all of Western literature if we are to follow its allusions and quotations. We are drawn out of the poem into a larger, more inclusive significance and pulled back to its striking concrete situations and musical virtuosity. More puzzling still, these often seem at odds, for if the constant juxtaposition of past and present suggests that we are dealing with the historic human condition or contrasting ourselves ironically to it, individual passages convincingly evoke a very personal and even private experience. "My nerves are bad to-night. Yes, bad. Stay with me," says a woman, and our attention is focused on a single room, a painful, intimate drama. And if Tiresias's distanced and world-weary observations generalize the banality of lust, the unnamed narrator's cry, "O City city," has the sound of authentic and individual longing.

Is *The Waste Land,* then, one poem or many, a lyric expression of personal emotion or an impersonal comment on contemporary civilization and history's repetitions? Any reading of it must begin with these questions, and before they can be answered, we must understand the source of these disparate and conflicting forms and perspectives.

The Waste Land was composed from a series of many poems and fragments written over several years. The story of its creation is fascinating in itself, a modern mystery with a missing manuscript, hidden clues, and surprising discoveries. Although the published poem is the completed work of art and the text we read and study, we can no longer entirely separate it from the material that went into it and the effects of the editing process that produced it. Nor can we understand the sources and selective process until we have traced the story back to its beginnings.

Eliot himself created the mystery. On 19 July 1922 he wrote to John Quinn, a New York lawyer and art collector who had admired and supported Eliot's work, that he wished to send Quinn a gift:

> I should like to present you the MSS of the Waste Land, if you would care to have it—when I say MSS, I mean that it is partly MSS and partly typescript, with Ezra's and my alterations scrawled all over it.[4]

He added later that he thought the manuscript worth preserving as evidence of the effect of Ezra Pound's criticism. Quinn received the manuscript in January 1923 and acknowledged it on 26 February. But when he died in 1924, it was not mentioned in his will and appeared to have been lost.

The published poem became the subject of an enormous quantity of commentary and interpretation. Books, articles, and reviews poured out, defining its structure, tracking down its allusions, defining its modernism, and discussing its meaning and mood. But even as readers and critics offered explanations of the poem's unity and the poet's intentions, there were clues that a major piece of the puzzle was missing. In 1950 a series of letters, written by Pound and Eliot in 1921 and 1922, were published. They revealed that *The Waste Land* had been cut and edited from a much longer manuscript and that Pound had made major decisions about the final form. Asked in a *Paris Review* interview in 1959 whether the original manuscript existed, Eliot replied that he did not know but that whole sections had been cut. Without the original version, however, the nature of the cuts and changes could not be determined.

In October 1968 the New York Public Library announced that its Berg Collection had acquired the original manuscript of *The Waste Land,* and in 1971 a facsimile edition, including Pound's annotations, was published. This extraordinary discovery altered all interpretations of the poem and answered many questions: the fate of the manuscript since Quinn's death, the part played by Pound in the text's creation, and the range of materials combined and reordered into one poem.

The manuscripts had formed part of the estate inherited by John Quinn' sister. When she died in 1934, her husband and daughter put Quinn's papers in storage, where they remained until the early 1950s. The daughter, after a long search, found the manuscript of *The Waste Land* and in 1958 sold it to the Berg Collection. But for some reason the acquisition was not made public for ten years; even Eliot was not informed. Thus its sudden appearance caused both surprise and great interest.

What the manuscript reveals is that Eliot and Pound together worked from a mass of materials written at various times over several years. Although the bulk of the published poem was written in 1921, it includes lines and passages from much earlier material. The earliest fragments, which date from 1914, are three poems entitled "After the turning of the inspired days," "I am the Resurrection and the Life," and "So through the evening, through the violet air." Lines and images from "So through the evening" appear in "What the Thunder Said," and "After the turning of the inspired days" is an early version of the opening of that section. In 1915 Eliot wrote a poem called "The Death of St. Narcissus," which was not separately published until it was included in *Poems Written in Early Youth* in 1967. A section of "The Burial of the Dead" is drawn from it. Between 1916 and 1919 Eliot wrote a series of other poems and fragments inspired by London, his new work at Lloyd's Bank, and his marriage in 1915. They include a long poem called "The Death of the Duchess," which includes scenes and lines later incorporated into "A Game of Chess." The original manuscript contains both the early fragments and several miscellaneous poems.

In 1919 Eliot wrote to his mother that his New Year's resolution was "to write a long poem I have had on my mind for a long time."[5] He mentioned again, in a letter to her on 20 September 1920, that he longed for "a period of tranquility to do a poem that I have in mind."[6] During these years Eliot's personal life was extremely troubling and his professional life exhausting. His wife was often ill, their marriage was difficult, and he had to write his poetry and criticism after long days of work at Lloyd's Bank. In September 1921 he was granted a three-month leave for rest and medical treatment. He left London to undergo treatment in Margate and Lausanne for what he described as an "aboulie and emotional derangement." During the following three months he wrote the longest part of *The Waste Land*.

That his physical and emotional condition at the time acted as a kind of trigger for transforming private experience into poetry is apparent from many of his later comments on poetic creation. In a lecture at Harvard in 1933, later published in *The Use of Poetry and the Use of Criticism,* he spoke of the link between writing and illness:

> I know, for instance, that some forms of ill-health, debility or anaemia, may (if other circumstances are favourable) produce an efflux

of poetry in a way approaching the condition of automatic writing—though, in contrast to the claims sometimes made for the latter, the material has obviously been incubating within the poet, and cannot be suspected of being a present from a friendly or impertinent demon. What one writes in this way may succeed in standing the examination of a more normal state of mind; it gives me the impression, as I have just said, of having undergone a long incubation, though we do not know until the shell breaks what kind of egg we have been sitting on.[7]

Other comments made at different times support this suggestion that *The Waste Land* was a release of long-held feelings and emotionally charged images that came together during his release from work and tension. In the *Paris Review* interview, for example, he said that his purpose in writing the poem was to get something off his chest. And in "The Three Voices of Poetry" (1953) he spoke of a poet who may be concerned only with expressing an obscure impulse:

He is oppressed by a burden which he must bring to birth in order to obtain relief. Or, to change the figure of speech, he is haunted by a demon, a demon against which he feels powerless, because in its first manifestation it has no face, no name, nothing; and the words, the poem he makes, are a kind of form of exorcism of this demon. In other words again, he is going to all that trouble, not in order to communicate with anyone, but to gain relief from acute discomfort[8]

The emotions, feelings, dreams, and experiences of several years apparently fused in the material written during 1921.

When Eliot returned to London in January 1922, he stopped over for a few days in Paris, where he submitted the manuscript to Pound's editing. At Pound's suggestion he cut three long descriptive passages and all the miscellaneous poems and separate fragments, leaving the five sections of the published poem. He also cut or rewrote many lines.

Thus *The Waste Land* as it was published in 1922 contained varied parts of poems originally not conceived of as a single poem but arranged as one. To add to that complexity, the notes added a mass of

information and allusion that had to be incorporated into an under-
standing of it. The notes were not originally a part of the poem, which
was first published in two periodicals—the *Dial* and the *Criterion*—
without them. They were added to the first edition in book form, ac-
cording to Eliot, because "it was discovered that the poem was incon-
veniently short, so I set to work to expand the notes, in order to
provide a few more pages of printed matter."[9] But regardless of the
intention, they had the effect of directing the reader's attention away
from immediate experience of the poem toward a historical context
and symbolic meaning. We are to recognize that the dressing table of
the neurotic woman in "A Game of Chess" has something in common
with Cleopatra's barge, that the song in the opening of "The Fire Ser-
mon" comes from Spenser's *Prothalamion,* that the empty chapel in
"What the Thunder Said" refers to the Perilous Chapel of the Grail
legends as interpreted by Jessie Weston. Even the most direct personal
emotion, the loss and regret in the Hyacinth garden, is referred by
allusion to Joseph Conrad's *Heart of Darkness* and to *Tristan und
Isolde.* Is it, then, to be read as the voice of a sensitive consciousness
recalling a missed experience? Or is it a collocation of representative
stories viewed ironically from a distance as expressions of contempo-
rary existence?

In a sense, the poem is both, and more; it is built up in layers of
different themes and styles that coalesce in an enigmatic, complicated
relation. If we read the published poem on its own, seeking a single
way of accounting for its contradictions, we can do so only by ignor-
ing or eliminating or subordinating much of what it contains. But a
study of the original manuscript can reveal both the many layers of
material and the very different passages originally considered part of
the whole and then removed to leave scenes and moods and feelings
less clearly accounted for. Though there was never a logical sequence,
the passages we now read were often embedded in a context of more
explanatory or thematic material. The history of the poem thus helps
direct our understanding of its meaning.

The original manuscript of *The Waste Land,* which Eliot brought
home from Lausanne, was more than twice as long as the published

version. The material that was cut from the poem is, if anything, more varied in style and mood than what was kept. Much of it is satire or parody. It includes narrative, dramatic scenes, and lyrics; blank verse, heroic couplets, iambic tetrameter, and free verse. Like the published poem, it had no formal intellectual pattern. Eliot himself, when asked whether the cutting and editing had changed "the intellectual structure of the poem," replied that he thought it "was just as structureless, only in a more futile way, in the longer version."[10]

The longer version, however, did have a different title—*He Do the Police in Different Voices*—taken from Charles Dickens's *Our Mutual Friend*. In chapter 16 an old woman named Betty Higden remarks of Sloppy, a foundling whom she has adopted, "You mightn't think it, but Sloppy is a beautiful reader of a newspaper. He do the police in different voices." The title we are familiar with suggests a vision of a land in trouble: it calls for a unified meaning or structure. But the first title made no such suggestion; it offered instead a medley of voices interpreted by a single voice. Reading the poem with the expectation of such a medley, we would be less surprised at its shifts and changes.

Although the manuscript does not show the dates when each section was written, it is clear that the five sections of the published poem were composed in 1921, probably from October to December.[11] When he went to Margate, Eliot took with him the older fragments and possibly the first part of "The Fire Sermon," a parody of Alexander Pope that describes a young woman preoccupied with trivial society and vulgar sex, and under the delusion that she is a poet. The tone is both crude and harshly satiric. Like many of the fragments written from 1916 to 1919, this passage focused on the urban landscape and social life of London. Though this focus is lost in the published poem, much of the imagery and sense of horror at London life remains in new contexts, especially an unease with women and sexual relations.

While Eliot was in Margate and Lausanne on his three months' leave, he completed *The Waste Land*. Like "The Fire Sermon," "The Burial of the Dead" and "Death by Water" originally had long narrative openings. The opening of "The Burial of the Dead" portrayed a night out on the town in a sleazy section of Boston. The narrator visits a bar, the Opera Exchange, and the German Club. A companion describes his visit to a brothel where he was too drunk to get a woman. "Death by Water" opened with a long description of a shipwreck, sailors lured to their death by sirens. Both of these are told in the first person, and they are realistic and dramatic. Moreover, both are set in America: Boston and the Atlantic off New England. Although Eliot's interest in London life dominated the fragments written immediately preceding his departure, he shifted to memories of his American past for the next sections of the poem. By cutting these passages, Pound and Eliot made the poem again European.

It is with sections 1 and 2 that the original title appears, suggesting that a long poem in a variety of styles and situations was the aim. What is especially interesting about these poems is that they are told as vivid personal memories. In "The Burial of the Dead" the narrator seeks out a vulgar sensuality on which he elsewhere looks with weary revulsion or satiric detachment. In "Death by Water" the sailor who dies tells his own story of fear and horror. At this stage of writing the poem, Eliot's focus seems to have shifted from satire to personal memory and experience presented in long narrative passages. The imagistic and suggestive passages that now open both sections originally followed these narratives. It is significant that up to this point the poem included little or nothing to suggest the broader symbolic structure presented by the notes. Rather, these narratives are concrete, realistic, full of specific and precise detail about streets and pubs and ships and people who live in them—a man named Joe singing "I'm proud of all the Irish blood that's in me," Myrtle who runs the brothel, "little Ben Levin the tailor," and a sailor who limps with a "comic gonorrhea."

In addition to parts of the five sections constituting the published poem, ten pieces in varying styles and on varying themes were suppressed. Of these, some resemble sections and styles that were retained. "The Death of the Duchess," like the opening of "The Fire Sermon," is urban and satiric. "So through the evening, through the violet air" resembles sections of "What the Thunder Said." And "Dirge" is a satiric alternative version of "Death by Water." In selecting and arranging from this material, Pound and Eliot to some extent chose what was poetically most effective. But they also changed the emphasis of the poem. Poems like "The Death of St. Narcissus" and "Song" express very personal emotions and fears, and the story of Phlebas has a different significance when placed immediately after the story of New England fishermen drawn to their death by singing women than when it is set off alone.

If a poem is written as a single unified structure, whether narrative, dramatic, lyric, or satiric, each part has a specific relation to the next and to the whole. But a poem composed of disparate pieces, selected and arranged, not only alters in its meaning as a whole with any change in position or inclusion but alters in each part. An individual passage changes its implication depending on context. In *The Waste Land* the changing thematic focus is further complicated by changes in style. Although the style was varied throughout, satire dominated in the material of 1916–1919 and "The Fire Sermon." Much of the deleted narrative material was more personal and direct than what was retained. And the fifth section, written last, is primarily surreal, symbolic, and meditative. It is only with this section that the overarching symbolic pattern suggested by the notes seems very apparent. And with its addition, the preceding poems can seem to take on a new and larger range of meaning than they have either in themselves or as a group. Lines, phrases, and images take on new suggestive value in light of the conclusion. For example, the opening scenes of "What the Thunder Said" depict Christ's arrest and death on the cross. Reading the earlier sections with that in mind can create a sense that the narrator longs throughout the poem for a Christian faith. Similarly, the theme of the Perilous Chapel, which Eliot's notes define as part of "What the Thunder Said," refers to the story of a knight in quest of the Grail and can suggest the presence of a questing figure from the beginning. Yet, in itself, the opening would not give this impression.

The Waste Land, then, is many poems arranged into a pattern. But because the parts are so varied, the pattern does not unify and organize the material into a single meaning. It provides instead a framework within which many complex themes and moods interact.

Nor can the pattern account for all that it includes. That is, many feelings are expressed in the published poem for which the actual scenes and events do not provide clear reasons. Though the prevailing mood of despair and regret seems to exceed the situations that evoke it, clearer reasons are often present in parts of the original manuscript. The withdrawn and enigmatic man of "A Game of Chess" who responds to his companion's hysteria with disconnected fragments of speech expresses his fears overtly in "The Death of the Duchess": "And if I said 'I love you' should we breath/ . . . If I said 'I do not love you' we should breathe." The persistent fear of women is made explicit in the original opening of "The Fire Sermon." The sources of horror and fear that run through the published poem are named in poems like "The Death of St. Narcissus" and "Elegy,"which describe guilt and remorse at sexual experience and the wish for a loved one to stay dead.

What remains in the published poem is a set of moods, often without concrete bases in situation or event, along with dramatic scenes and stream-of-consciousness meditations on desire, sexuality, loss, life and death, and the possibility of change, hope, and restoration of value.

Yet these disparate pieces do coalesce into a kind of whole. The whole may be defined as an emotional consistency, a conception of history, or a mythic structure. Each definition focuses on specific relations within the composed pattern of individual poems. Our experience of this challenging and yet exciting poem is ultimately a composite of responses to its many layers of mood, theme, and image.

5

Structure and Theme

"The Burial of the Dead" opens with a curious and disturbing image of lilacs growing out of dead land. It closes with an image of a dog digging up human bones in a garden. In between it moves from an Austrian countess's memories of childhood in the mountains to scenes of desert heat and drought to a moment of young desire in a garden of hyacinths to a fortune-teller and a scene of London streets crowded with lonely, empty people. Although these distinct scenes and characters seem at first to have little to do with one another, they are linked not only by a prevailing mood of fear, loss, and unease but by formal patterns. Here and throughout the five parts of *The Waste Land* several techniques create a framework and a kind of unity. Of these, the most important are a classification of images and experience, musical patterns of repetition and variation, a central consciousness, and a major theme emerging in many forms and continuously elaborated upon.

CLASSIFICATION

The classification of images and experience appears at once in those opening and closing lines of the first section, which dwell on things buried in the earth—roots, dried tubers, rocks, dead bones—or growing from it—lilacs, branches, hyacinths, corpses. Images of earth fill the first section as images of air, fire, and water fill the sections that follow. The titles of three of these sections point to the categories of earth, fire, and water: "The Burial of the Dead," "The Fire Sermon," and "Death by Water." "A Game of Chess" does not suggest air, but the original title of that section was "In the Cage," an image of hanging in air. While images of all four elements recur across sections, the element noted in the title provides a central image in each section around which scenes cluster.

In addition to the specific images of burial in earth and growing out of earth, "The Burial of the Dead" returns in all but the Madame Sosostris passage to images of land and soil. Marie remembers the mountains; the narrator speaks of "fear in a handful of dust"; the German sailor sings of wind that blows to the homeland (*Der Heimat zu*); the crowds in London stare at the street before their feet; the dog digs in the dirt. Mountains, deserts, rocks, gardens, and streets provide the specific locations for each scene.

In "A Game of Chess" the scene has moved indoors to a lady's dressing room and a pub. Persistent images of smells and smoke and wind refer us to presences in the air. The wind, especially, forms a key part of the conversation in the first section as the tense and urgent woman asks "What is that noise?" and is told, "The wind under the door," and again asks, "What is the wind doing?" Air stirs the perfumes and odors. More pervasively still, the section is characterized by voices in the air: the nightingale's song, the conversations, the "Shakespeherian rag," the sound of the barman's call. "A Game of Chess" closes with the woman in the pub echoing Ophelia's mad song.

"The Fire Sermon" is not so obviously focused on fire. In fact, images of the River Thames and the wind are more prominent, with fire appearing overtly only in the last lines: "Burning, burning, burning, burning." In this case we can find the significance of fire only by reference to the source of the title and to the line, "To Carthage then I came." The title comes from Buddha's fire sermon, preached against the fires of passion, hate, and infatuation. The line, from St. Augustine's *Confessions*, is part of the longer line, "to Carthage then I came, where a cauldron of unholy lusts sang all about my ears." Once we see that the "fire" is a metaphor for lust, we recognize that the entire section is based in it. "The Fire Sermon" depicts a series of casual and empty sexual encounters, from brief liaisons between the nymphs and loitering heirs of city directors to Sweeney and Mrs. Porter, the typist and "the young man carbuncular," and the Thames-daughters. The final word, "burning," is a kind of summing up.

"Death by Water" takes place in the sea. Although in the published poem it consists of a brief lyric on the drowning of Phlebas, the original manuscript included a long narrative of a shipwreck. In both versions the sea is the central focus.

Because there are only four elements, Eliot could not sustain that classification throughout the poem. Instead he added a culminating section, developing the themes and images begun in the earlier parts. "What the Thunder Said" is a kind of response to the questioning and desire of the first four sections. Images from the previous sections recur: the dry rock, the wind, the sea, and water as rain and a spring among the rocks. Fire in the form of lust is not directly present although there are lighted torches and lightning, but the thunder's admonitions are alternative responses to human relationship. Giving, sympathizing, and controlling contrast to the self-absorbed and uncontrolled gratification of lust depicted in "The Fire Sermon."

Earth, air, fire, and water are not only formal categories: they constitute the physical world. And in one sense *The Waste Land* is an emotional response to the physical world, to the meaning of physical experience and life in the world. Eliot's earlier poetry portrayed a sad and ugly but often touching world of city streets and fog and wind blowing across empty lots, yet he also sustained a mood of longing for spiritual significance, for a world of meaning outside ordinary human experience. That mood permeates *The Waste Land* as well. The world of earth, air, fire, and water is a world of death and sorrow, a world needing restoration.

As we have seen in the case of fire, however, the elements can function metaphorically as well as literally. Earth is not only literal rocks and soil; it represents both generation and death, breeding and decay. Thus, memory and desire as well as roots and corpses are buried and stirred by April. Air is manifested as both transfiguring song in the voice of the swallow and madness in the song of Ophelia. Fire, which refers throughout "The Fire Sermon" to the sterile burning of lust, recalls also, in the poem's conclusion, the fire of purgation. Water as the destructive sea transforms eyes to pearls and as rain relieves the dead land.

The Music of Poetry

Within the five larger sections of *The Waste Land* are shorter, separable units or verse paragraphs. They consist of scenes, meditations, satiric comments, descriptions, lyric passages, and sometimes quotations alone. While these scenes and styles are extremely varied, the verse form is fairly consistent. It is made up of verse paragraphs in different lengths with a predominantly iambic rhythm, or alternating unstressed and stressed syllables. Eliot frequently begins or ends a line with an extra syllable or reversed stress, but the line usually returns to the dominant rhythm, as in this passage:

> What are the roots that clutch, what branches grow
> Out of this stony rubbish? Son of man,

or this:

> a crowd flowed over London Bridge, so many,
> I had not thought death had undone so many.

Although the rhythm is very loosely iambic and seldom appears as a consistent metric pattern as it does, for example, in "A Game of

Chess" or the typist episode, it sustains a recurrent familiar musical sound. Thus an underlying pattern remains throughout despite the freedom of paragraph length and lack of rhyme.

But the rhythm of poetry is not a matter of sound alone. In a 1942 essay entitled "The Music of Poetry" Eliot defined that music as twofold, having to do with meaning as well as sound. "But I believe that the properties in which music concerns the poet most nearly, are the sense of rhythm and the sense of structure." His purpose, he claims, "is to insist that a 'musical poem' is a poem which has a musical pattern of sound and a musical pattern of the secondary meanings of the words which compose it, and that these two patterns are indissoluble and one."[12]

The idea of a musical pattern of sound is familiar enough; it has to do with a recurrent beat or sequence of sounds. A musical pattern of words is, likewise, the repetition and variation of key words, phrases, and ideas. Poetry tends to create much of its effect by such repetitions. Eliot uses them consistently in all his poetry, including *The Waste Land,* to hold together disparate material. In *The Waste Land* he uses such links in several ways, including an opening introduction of characters who reappear, repeated words and images, clusters of images linked to a dominant element, and the recurrence of key passages.

In "The Burial of the Dead" Madame Sosostris, in her role as fortune-teller, introduces a series of characters: the Phoenician Sailor, Belladonna, the man with three staves, the one-eyed merchant, the Hanged Man, and crowds of people walking in a ring. All reappear in the poem, especially the Phoenician Sailor, who is identified with the narrator and who is associated with the image of pearls as eyes. An entire section is also devoted to his drowning. Belladonna, "the lady of situations," reappears as all the women of the poem and the man with three staves as the Fisher King. The merchant is Mr. Eugenides, and the crowds walk the streets of London. Although Madame Sosostris cannot find the Hanged Man, he is linked to Christ in section 5.

Although the characters introduced by Madame Sosostris are not the only ones in the poem, they act as primary representatives of the human condition as Eliot portrays it—the lost empty crowds, the betrayed and betraying women, the sensitive, seeking figure who is transformed through death or may be, the potentially restoring god. In one sense, Eliot tells us in the note to line 218, all the characters are united into one in Tiresias, who had been both male and female and who had the gift of prophecy. Madame Sosostris's cards foretell not only individuals but the forms of experience present throughout the poem. The entire poem, then, is a set of variations on the themes she introduces.

Images as well as characters recur throughout the poem. As we have seen, images of earth, air, fire, and water dominate sections but also reappear not only in section 5 but in each section. While rain is awaited throughout the entire poem, the summer arrives in the first paragraph "With a shower of rain." The hyacinth girl's hair is wet. The wind blows across the brown land in "The Fire Sermon." "Those are pearls that were his eyes," a line alluding to a sea change, appears in sections 1 and 2. And Lil and her friend suggest the fire of lust as much as any figures in "The Fire Sermon." While each of the first four sections focuses on an element, the images are linked across sections. That this linkage is deliberate is evident from the notes where Eliot several times points out connections: the repetition of the "pearls" image, the recurrence of rats in the alley and creeping on the river bank, and the song of Philomela.

Other key images also recur within and between sections. Hair is both sensual and disturbing. The hyacinth girl comes back from the Hyacinth garden with arms full and hair wet. But the woman of "A Game of Chess" brushes her hair out "in fiery points," an image of nervous tension, and the woman in "What the Thunder Said" draws "her long black hair out tight." The typist merely "smoothes her hair with automatic hand."

The songs of birds likewise modulate from the crude " 'Jug Jug' to dirty ears" to the "inviolable voice" and the water dripping song of the hermit thrush. The cry of the cock heralds the longed-for coming of rain. Plants, too, evoke changing moods: the lilacs of spring, the hyacinths of young desire, the dusty trees and dry grass of sterility and lost desire. Bodies, dead or lying on the ground or "Supine on the floor of a narrow canoe," bones in a garret or on the sea floor, pearls, rats, voices singing, and churches rising above the degraded streets, all evoke in different contexts changing moods and responses to desire, generation, and death.

Encountering these repeated images is like hearing a musical motif repeated in different settings: we feel both familiarity and surprise. The many kinds of material Eliot brings together in the poem seem, as we read, to bring us back, over and over, to the same feelings and ideas. An emotional consistency remains in changing situations. In some cases, this is made more overt by the recurrence of longer scenes or ideas. Both "The Burial of the Dead" and "What the Thunder Said" open with scenes of desert and rock. Thus a kind of cyclic pattern is set up. The coming of rain, certain or possible, occurs at the beginning and end. The "Unreal City" of the first section collapses in the last: "What is the city over the mountains / Cracks and reforms and bursts in the violet air / Falling towers." Most important, perhaps, the voice of the thunder seems to answer the questions implicit in the entire poem—whether and how human relations can be genuine and fruitful and life therefore have value.

THE CENTRAL CONSCIOUSNESS

The Waste Land, while it has no overall logical or narrative structure, has the unity of related situations and experiences as well as regular patterns of recurrence. All of the characters live in a world without love, relationship, action, or religion, where nothing fulfills and desire fails. But it is not their plight alone that moves us. Despite the many voices and shifting scenes, we sense a central consciousness whose perspective colors all we perceive and whose longing and despair most deeply affect us. Many readers of the poem have seen a kind of plot in which a single figure seeks to find an answer and restore value. While it is difficult to identify such a figure, whose identity rests in a continuous quest, there is a dominant point of view, a way of perceiving the world, which is identified with the unnamed narrator, who speaks more often and more continuously than anyone else.

One way of thinking about the characters of *The Waste Land* is suggested by Lyndall Gordon. "Eliot's characters are not as realistic as Pound's," she says. "They are projections of Eliot's haunted consciousness."[13] Gordon demonstrates the autobiographical sources of much of the poem and sees the "meditative voice" as Eliot's. Although she does not point to a single central voice, the medley of many voices is, she claims, contrived, "for the meditative voice is never truly submerged."[14] Gordon's interpretation is helpful, for if we examine the many characters and voices, we find that all are viewed through a single mood and perspective. They do not represent different or contrasting ways of understanding the world but rather form many ways of illustrating the same perceptions.

Eliot's original title suggests what Gordon defines. *He Do the Police in Different Voices* refers both to the many voices of the newspaper accounts and to Sloppy's ability to imitate them. All the voices of the newspaper are, in one sense, Sloppy's voice, since he interprets them and colors them with his own voice. In another sense, they are the voices of London that happen to be in any given newspaper. In like manner, Lil and Marie, Madame Sosostris and Tiresias, speak for themselves, but what they say fits into the constant preoccupations of the narrator, illustrating them and projecting his sense of life into all of society. The characters never present an alternative worldview as they might in, say, a play by Shakespeare. *The Waste Land* is not a single story but a collection of stories interpreted through a single vision.

Although the narrator is never named or described, we know many things about him. First of all, the narrator is male. He appears as the husband in "A Game of Chess" and as a former soldier in "Burial of the Dead," and he is identified with the drowned Phoenician Sailor by Madame Sosostris. He speaks of himself as fishing twice, and the notes tell us that this image recalls the Fisher King. Secondly, he is upper-class or at least of the well-educated classes, as his knowledge of Western thought and literature reveals. We know also that he is fearful of sexuality, uneasy with women, and preoccupied with loss and a longing for spiritual significance. With the exception of Tiresias, nearly all the other voices are female, and they are defined and sometimes judged by the narrator. His meditations run through the entire poem, sometimes commenting on the action, as in "O City city," sometimes participating in it, as in the first scene of "A Game of Chess," sometimes meditating on its larger meaning, as in the openings of "The Burial of the Dead" and "The Fire Sermon."

In addition to the unnamed narrator, another character observes and comments on the London scene. As the typist encounters the carbuncular young man, Tiresias watches and reports. He claims, also, to have foretold and even experienced it all himself. Tiresias is unique, for he has been both male and female and was granted the gift of prophecy. Because of this, Eliot uses him as a figure who can incorporate all human experience—male and female, past and future. In the notes Eliot calls Tiresias the most important figure in the poem:

> Tiresias, although a mere spectator and not indeed a "character," is yet the most important personage in the poem, uniting all the rest. Just as the one-eyed merchant, seller of currants, melts into the Phoenician Sailor, and the latter is not wholly distinct from Ferdinand Prince of Naples, so all the women are one woman, and the two sexes meet in Tiresias. What Tiresias *sees*, in fact, is the substance of the poem.[15]

As with many of Eliot's notes, this can be both helpful and misleading. It does not mean that Tiresias is the central figure of the poem, but rather that he recognizes something fundamental to all experience. He is clearly distinct from the narrator, who is a "character," and who does not know all time and experience. What is significant in this comment on Tiresias is the emphasis on what he *sees*. What he observes is merely a commonplace casual sexual encounter. But he sees it as degraded, meaningless, devoid of love or purpose or even desire. And he identifies with both characters, claiming to have "foresuffered all." He, though old and wrinkled, remembers all, knowing it is all the same.

If we take Tiresias, then, as the central consciousness, the "substance" of the poem is the stale sameness of all failed human interaction. But it is difficult to read the poem in this way. The inclusiveness of Tiresias's vision differs from the perspective of the narrator, who is a part of the world Tiresias sees. Although Tiresias says that life is all the same, the narrator hopes, desires, and despairs at the lives lived around him. He does not identify with other women or men. Nonetheless, the weary sense of futility expressed by Tiresias defines the narrator's fear that everything is always all the same and that no alternative human world is possible. Tiresias serves to extend the narrator's immediate perceptions of life in London in the twentieth century into a universal vision of all time and all human experience, male and female.

The narrator's generalization of private experience is not limited to Tiresias's perceptions. From the first, the narrator insists on the inclusion of others in his sense of life. "The Burial of the Dead" closes with the urgent accusation: "You! hypocrite lecteur!—mon semblable,—mon frère!" (You! hypocrite reader!—my double,—my brother!) This direct address to the reader demands that we all acknowledge our complicity in whatever the narrator describes. He addresses the reader again in "Death by Water," calling on our recognition of a shared destiny: "O you who turn the wheel and look to windward, / Consider Phlebas, who was once handsome and tall as you." And the voice of the thunder in the last section is addressed to every creature—gods, demons, and humans. In his reactions the narrator includes us: "What have we given?" "We think of the key, each in his prison." "Your heart would have responded."

Throughout *The Waste Land* the voice of the narrator keeps coming back, coloring our perception of all the other characters and events and insisting on the universality of his vision. In Tiresias Eliot embodies that universality, claiming for him, through all time, the feelings and sensations of both a London typist and a coarse seducer. Yet it is the narrator who, reappearing, links those figures with the drowned sailor and the Thames-daughters. He is thus, despite Eliot's note, more important for our understanding of the poem and the relation of its many parts than the figure of Tiresias. His prevailing voice defines the meaning and value of all the episodes.

THE MAJOR THEME

In *The Waste Land* a central voice speaks for the mass of people who live lives of empty routine and emotional isolation. The world, for this narrator, is a dead land, a place of sterility and loss, yet one in which value might be possible. While he both participates in it and observes it, he also imagines another way to live. After promising to show "fear in a handful of dust," he shows potential love in the allusion to Tristan and Isolde and the hyacinth girl. After Tiresias's story, he walks past the fishmen who lounge at noon and the church of Magnus Martyr. He imagines the water dripping and the thrush singing. Yet he also returns and returns to a sense of uncertainty and fear, to betrayal and indifference, falling towers and broken fragments.

Clues to the poem's theme appear in the epigraph. It is taken from the *Satiricon* of Petronius (1st century A.D.) and refers to the Sibyl of Cumae. Sibyls were women who, like Tiresias, had prophetic power. The Cumaean Sibyl was beloved by Apollo, who offered her whatever she wished. Because she asked to live as many years as she had grains of sand in her hand but forgot to ask for youth, she grew older and more withered but could not die. The epigraph is spoken by a character who is drunkenly boasting that he has seen wonders:

> Nam Sibyllam quidem Cumis ego ipse oculis meis vidi in ampulla pendere, et cum illi pueri dicerent: Σίβυλλα τί Θέλεις; respondebat illa: ἀποθανεῖν Θέλω.
> [For once I saw with my very own eyes the Sibyl at Cumae hanging in a cage, and when the boys said to her, "Sibyl, what do you want?" she answered, "I want to die."]

While this specific passage points to a longing for death, what underlies it is a weary continuation of mere existence when health, activity, joy, and sensation have gone. For the Sibyl, life is a horror because it can never regain meaning. The passage is also an image of being isolated and trapped, an image that foreshadows all the poem's scenes of lonely, hopeless people. The epigraph prepares us for both the death-in-life of the characters we will encounter and the strange longing for and fear of death of which the narrator speaks. In one sense, then, the poem is about a longing for final death because life has become a kind of continuing death.

But the theme is more complicated than that. It is an exploration of the deepest feelings and thoughts that make life such a horror.

The manuscript version of *The Waste Land* had a different epigraph, which Eliot removed at the suggestion of Ezra Pound. It is taken from Joseph Conrad's *Heart of Darkness* and describes the death of Kurtz. Kurtz had gone into the interior of Africa filled with idealistic dreams of bringing civilization to the natives and had instead ravaged and killed them to get ivory. Marlow, the narrator of the story, hears his last words and believes them to be a judgment on his life:

> Did he live his life again in every detail of desire, temptation, and surrender during that supreme moment of complete knowledge? He cried in a whisper at some image, at some vision,—he cried out twice, a cry that was no more than a breath—"The horror! the horror!"[16]

Although Eliot accepted Pound's advice to remove the Conrad epigraph, he replied that it was "much the most appropriate I can find, and somewhat elucidative."[17] What it suggests is not weariness of life or desire for death but the significance of the moment of death. For Kurtz it is a moment of revelation, a recognition of what he had become. Eliot's intention to use it and his belief that it is "elucidative" suggests that the focus of *The Waste Land* is inner rather than outer, an exploration of the soul more than society.

But the poem also points to a broader social meaning. Eliot begins the notes by referring readers to two major sources: *The Golden Bough* by Sir James Frazer and *From Ritual to Romance* by Jessie Weston. *The Golden Bough* is a study of ancient myths and their relation to modern religion. The volumes Eliot especially notes describe rituals associated with the gods Adonis, Attis, and Osiris, whose deaths and rebirths were linked to the yearly cycle of seasons and the cyclic renewal of life. The story of Jesus parallels these ancient stories of death and rebirth. In *From Ritual to Romance* Jessie Weston argues that medieval legends of the Grail grew out of these early fertility rituals. Weston's book, Eliot claims, will help explain *The Waste Land*.

In the Grail stories, as Weston describes them, there is always a land that has been laid waste, made barren and sterile, by the illness or wounding of a king called the Fisher King. Weston attributes his name to the fact that fish are ancient symbols of life. There is also a knight in quest of the Holy Grail. He undergoes many difficult adventures, including a visit to a Perilous Chapel where strange and terrifying events occur. If he fulfills his quest and either asks or answers certain questions correctly, the king will be restored and the land renewed by the coming of rain. The Grail stories share with the ancient rituals the restoration of a waste land to life and fertility. By choosing the title for his poem from Weston's account of these myths, Eliot suggested a symbolic meaning. Twentieth-century Europe, and especially London, can be seen as a spiritual waste land where love, faith, and sexuality have been lost or degraded but where renewal might be possible. Seen in this way, *The Waste Land* can be understood as impersonal and symbolic, a commentary on the nature of modern life, and many readers have interpreted it in this way. Yet within that larger context the individual characters act out their private fears and desires, and it is the narrator who, returning over and over, defines the world as a dead land.

The Waste Land is a direct look at what attracts and appalls in human experience. It looks at the deepest fears, secrets, anguish, and desire of a speaker who finds in the world confirmations of those feelings. He resists life, longing for the warmth and forgetfulness of winter; he cannot respond to sensual desire, failing to speak to or see the hyacinth girl; he feels disgust and often loathing for the people around him and cannot love or even talk with his wife. He contemplates dead bodies, lust, rape, and abortion. Yet he also, unlike Kurtz, retains his sense of another life defined through ideals of connection, rebirth, and possibly religious values.

In a lecture at Harvard University Eliot looked back on the controversy over his poem and rejected traditional interpretations:

Various critics have done me the honour to interpret the poem in terms of criticism of the contemporary world, have considered it, indeed, as an important bit of social criticism. To me it was only the relief of a personal and wholly insignificant grouse against life; it is just a piece of rhythmical grumbling.[18]

Whether or not we accept Eliot's reduction of the poem —"just . . . grumbling," "insignificant"—we can acknowledge that it is a personal response to life, a vision of human experience seen through private emotion. The central theme is the specific character of that individual "grouse against life," the feeling that life has lost value and death would be release unless value is restored, and—more important—that the horror of life lies within. *The Waste Land* projects inner images of horror onto the landscape and society, images connected by the narrator's personal despair and longing as well as formal patterns of rhythm and content.

6

"The Burial of the Dead"

April is the cruelest month, breeding
Lilacs out of the dead land, mixing
Memory and desire, stirring
Dull roots with spring rain.
Winter kept us warm, covering
Earth in forgetful snow, feeding
A little life with dried tubers.

These are among the best-known and most-quoted opening lines in twentieth-century poetry. Reading them, we encounter a personal, meditative voice commenting on the most fundamental sign of life and hope—the rebirth of vegetation in spring. We are familiar with these images from a long tradition of poems celebrating spring and renewal, from Chaucer's "Aprill with his showres soote" and Shakespeare's "daisies pied and violets blue / And ladysmocks all silver-white" to William Carlos Williams's "Now the grass, tomorrow / the stiff curl of wildcarrot leaf" and Denise Levertov's May mornings that pass "bearing / each a leaflined basket / of wakening flowers." Yet this description of spring is strange and puzzling, a resistance to life and denial of hope or rebirth. The narrator's emotional response to the physical world is unease and withdrawal. It is almost a kind of mourning, not of death but of life.

"The Burial of the Dead" focuses more consistently than any other section on the narrator's own experience and feeling. All four verse paragraphs are spoken or reported by the unnamed "I," and all include memories of moments in his past. Thus we have, in the opening section of *The Waste Land,* a predominantly personal and individual expression of mood. Indeed, were we to read "The Burial of the Dead" by itself, we might well take it for a dramatic monologue similar to "The Love Song of J. Alfred Prufrock" or "Gerontion." How much the narrator is Eliot himself is unclear, although much of the material—such as the conversation with Marie—has biographical sources. But whether it is Eliot or a created character like Prufrock (though more fluid and changing) it has the continuity of persistent ideas, attitudes, and expressions. The voice of the narrator, though always recurring, is less prominent in other sections; nonetheless, it sets up the consciousness and mood that underlie the whole.

Moreover, the narrator's opening images of cruel spring define the theme of "The Burial of the Dead." Throughout this first section of *The Waste Land* the narrator is confronted by the necessity to respond to the pressure of life and growth linked to death and decay. April demands a choice, a decision to risk hope or to feel nothing and be safe. It is a choice determined by the sense that life is painful and hard, that desire will be frustrated or fulfillment illusory. This sense of a terrible longing and fear haunts the characters of Eliot's earlier poems as well. Prufrock, the lady of "Portrait of a Lady," the narrators of "Rhapsody on a Windy Night" and "La Figlia che Piange," and Gerontion wish to act but are afraid, or they make slight gestures only and withdraw.

"Gerontion" is especially significant as a comparison because Eliot thought to include it as a prelude to the rest of *The Waste Land* but dropped the idea on Pound's advice. His sense that it would serve as a preface, however, suggests that he considered it linked in subject to the material that did come together as one long poem. Had he included it, the presence of a single character with a name would have increased the emphasis on a central consciousness. But more important, the theme would have been more overtly defined. "Gerontion" depicts a life without action or commitment, human love or religious belief. Gerontion looks back on his life as a failure because he chose to do nothing and to reject experience. He is an old man, facing death without having lived.

Like Gerontion, the narrator at the opening of "The Burial of the Dead" sees life as sets of choices to risk action or be dead, and like Gerontion, he is afraid to choose life. But the poem opens not on the end of a failed life but with a meditation on the time of choice, a moment for which earth itself is filled with symbolic associations: it is the source of life and growth; humans, according to Genesis, were created from it; we are dust and return to dust; we bury the dead in the earth; and we bury also seeds that send forth branches and blossoms. Earth contains both life and death. Thus the narrator's first observations on the physical world are couched in the ambiguous union of possibility and loss.

Although most of "The Burial of the Dead" is spoken by the narrator, the voices he hears and recalls share his experience, enlarge, reinforce, and echo it. Marie, the sailor in *Tristan und Isolde,* the hyacinth girl, Madame Sosostris, and the crowds who sigh as they walk down King William Street all speak of death and desire. His voice continually yields to, responds to, and incorporates those of others. He remembers voices speaking to him and fragments or phrases he has read or heard about love and death, hope and loss, from the Bible, Baudelaire, Dante, Webster, Wagner. If we look at "The Burial of the Dead" as a whole we find several voices addressing similar questions, questions introduced at the outset by the narrator and linked by his recurring voice. It is his mood that colors all the incidents.

Looking more closely at the opening, we find that it is both complex and moving in its presentation. It consists of two sentences of four lines and three lines. The first three lines are constructed alike with a pause before the last word and a slight rise on the "ing" with which each ends. The reader is forced to pause and draw out the verbs that express April's cruelty, its insistence on breeding, mixing, stirring.

The sentence ends in line four on the word "rain," the stimulus of this new generation. Lines five through eight repeat the pattern with contrasting end words, suggesting not awakening but quiescence: "covering," "feeding," "tubers." Spring arouses; winter hides and keeps.

Other contrasts appear with the basic one of action and passivity—wet/dry, memory/forgetfulness, desire/a little life. Memory and desire connect past and future, making the present a time of awareness and choice. Winter allows forgetting and sustains a kind of blankness without need to think or choose. The judgment of spring and winter gives way to a specific memory of summer:

> Summer surprised us, coming over the Starnbergersee
> With a shower of rain; we stopped in the colonnade,
> And went on in sunlight, into the Hofgarten,
> And drank coffee, and talked for an hour.

The surprise of summer is not explained. It may have come suddenly or it may have been different from what was expected. In any case, it is unlike both spring and winter, neither painful nor devoid of awareness. The rain that is absent from the rest of the poem falls and passes on, leaving sunlight and an hour of talk with an acquaintance. The voice seems to shift at this point with the phrase in German, Marie's assurance that she is not Russian but comes from Lithuania and is pure German. The speaker is now Countess Marie Larisch, niece and confidante of the Austrian Empress Elizabeth, with whom Eliot had once met and talked. According to Valerie Eliot, the conversation is taken verbatim from theirs.

Marie recalls her childhood and a moment when she conquered fear, daring to go downhill on a sled. But she has changed: she reads all night and goes south in winter, leaving the mountains she claims make you feel free. Her memories focus on winter, which once was exciting and now keeps her warm. Yet the scene as a whole is ambiguous, for although the narrator and Marie both express fear of life and a wish to keep warm and quiet, they do something here that does not appear again in the poem: they talk for an hour in a public park in summer. Marie is confidential and revealing; she seems to sense a sympathetic listener to whom she can tell her memories, feelings, and present restlessness.

The opening passage of "The Burial of the Dead" sets up the key themes of the whole poem. In the rest of the first section they are replayed in a series of scenes between the narrator and other characters. His own memories and the experiences and memories of those he meets focus on responses to desire and death. In the second passage, for example, two opposing scenes occur, divided by a song about young love. The first is a desert land: dry, hot, dead, and fearful. The second is a garden in spring: rain-soaked, blooming, the location of intimacy. Twice a quotation from Wagner's *Tristan und Isolde* intervenes, first a song of love and longing, then a line about lost love. Both the geography of dead land and gardens and the concern with literal and symbolic seasons connect the second passage to the first.

The voice of the second passage has altered, become urgently questioning and authoritative, yet it still speaks as "I" and comes back to the images of roots and branches and dead land. This time it is summer without rain, summer as drought and death, and the language is prophetic. Eliot begins in this scene the interweaving of allusion and quotation with the narrator's speech, drawing on the Old Testament for the scene of desolation and tone of warning. He brings together phrases from Ezekiel and Ecclesiastes with slightly altered lines from the early unpublished poem "The Death of St. Narcissus." The function of allusion is complex and will be discussed in a later chapter, but its most immediate effect, if we recognize the source, is to extend the range of meaning in a given line or image; that is, the vision of the narrator enlarges to include that of the work to which he refers: it may intensify, add to, or ironically contrast with his own situation and experience. In this case, the opening personal voice takes on a broader authority by its incorporation of biblical prophecy.

In the first six lines of the second passage Eliot weaves in two references to Ezekiel and one to Ecclesiastes. In the first, he recalls the phrase "Son of Man," God's name for Ezekiel. God called on Ezekiel to take his word to the Israelites but warned that they would not listen. In Ezekiel 6:4 he tells Ezekiel to warn them that their "altars shall be desolate, and [their] images shall be broken," and he then warns them that their cities shall be laid waste and that many will die because of their idolatry. In Ecclesiastes God calls on the people to remember him in the days of their youth because the time will come when "fears shall be in the way, and the almond tree shall flourish, and the grasshopper shall be a burden, and desire shall fail: because man goeth to his long home, and the mourners go about the streets" (Ecclesiastes 12:5). Eliot picks up the "Son of Man," the "broken images," and the rhythms and images of Ecclesiastes in the dead tree and cricket and dry stone. He also uses lines a little further on in Ecclesiastes 12:7 saying that after all this, "Then shall the dust return to the earth as it was." Dead land, broken images, the sound of the cricket, fear and dust, all take on the significance of human failure and prophetic warning from the biblical references.

Yet there is a difference between the narrator's vision and the biblical desolation. The narrator has asked what can clutch or grow out of the dead land, and the prophetic voice is denied knowledge or power to say:

> Son of man,
> You cannot say, or guess, for you know only
> A heap of broken images . . .

And yet he offers to provide an answer in the handful of dust. The lines are enigmatic, but they suggest that the fear of which he speaks is in some way darker, more terrible even than the prophet's warning. What it is is not explained, and, in fact, the poem is full of a sense of terror that is never fully accounted for. Its presence is a constant disturbing background to every scene. There is in this passage, however, another kind of "allusion" to Eliot's own early work. Since "The Death of St. Narcissus" was never published by Eliot except privately, appearing first in 1967 in *Poems Written in Early Youth*, Eliot did not intend the reference to be recognized. But the lines on the red rock and shadow and handful of dust are drawn from a poem in which the central figure feels a kind of horror of himself. Because of his imagined images of himself as degraded and caught in perverse sexuality and violence, he goes out into the desert to die, making explicit the link between dry land and death reinvoked in all of "The Burial of the Dead." It is as if those imaginings inform the narrator's unexplained sense of horror though no reason is clearly given in this poem. And he claims a deeper and more profound understanding of the waste and sorrow he beholds than even the prophet he invokes.

The desert scene of heat and fear and death is abruptly dropped, and a song from Wagner's *Tristan und Isolde* intervenes. A sailor sings of his longing for the girl he has left behind. This lyric of innocent, unself-conscious love heightens by contrast the constraint of the narrator or Marie. It serves both to suggest an alternative to their fears and to introduce a new scene of spring and potential love. Eliot's quick scene changes often play off one another, highlighting moods by contrast. The scene of the hyacinth girl shares both the moment of intimacy and trust and the subsequent fear and withdrawal of Marie's memories; coming after the desert images of death and the sailor's song, it conflates their meanings of possibility and loss.

The episode of the hyacinth girl has been called the most important of the poem. According to one commentator, for example, it reveals "the personal predicament at the heart of the poem."[19] Another defines it as the key to the whole: "At the center of 'The Burial of the Dead,' and at the center of the nightmare of *The Waste Land*, lies the episode of the Hyacinth garden."[20] What distinguishes this scene and gives it its aura of profound significance is that it is the only moment of deep intimacy and communication in the poem. Although Marie and the narrator talk confidentially together, their relationship is brief and casual. The hyacinth girl seems moved by a more intense and serious encounter, and the narrator's diction associates it with universal questions of life and death.

Hyacinths bloom early in spring. With the quoted words of the hyacinth girl we are back in the time and location of memory and desire. She recalls the previous spring when the narrator met her in a garden wet with spring rain and gave her flowers, a gesture with accepted connotations of attraction or love. It names her as one associated with the stirring of life and beauty: "They called me the hyacinth girl." He seems to have given flowers more than once, since she says "first," and she speaks of that time a year later. But he recalls something else, a response set in contrast by the "yet":

> —Yet when we came back, late, from the Hyacinth garden,
> Your arms full, and your hair wet, I could not
> Speak, and my eyes failed, I was neither
> Living nor dead, and I knew nothing,
> Looking into the heart of light, the silence.

Despite his recognition of feeling, he acts out the perception in the opening lines, the sense that life is too cruel to acknowledge. He is impotent in the face of desire. But he couches his disability in exaggerated terms; he has lost all sensation, knows nothing, faces some ultimate silence. The moment in the Hyacinth garden takes on for him a meaning beyond itself. It represents a fundamental response to the world and to others, the withdrawal into self and solitude. This is suggested not only by the reiteration of images from the description of April and winter—water, flower, life and death—but the inversion of "heart of darkness." For Conrad, the heart of darkness is within. But when Marlow meets Kurtz's fiancée, he recognizes in her the light of great belief in the ideal. In a darkening room, light gathers around her forehead, and she seems to represent all possibility for faith and hope. Here the narrator looks into the "heart of light" and is left without speech or sight, life or death. In a moment of possible fulfillment of potential human love, he cannot respond or act at all.

The Hyacinth garden episode depicts a moment of decision between engaging in life or holding back, and the narrator cannot choose life. It closes with another line from *Tristan und Isolde*, "*Oed' und leer das Meer*" (Waste and empty the sea), spoken by a lookout who watches for Isolde's ship. Tristan, dying, waits for her, but no ship is coming. Thus the framing lines from Wagner set the Hyacinth garden scene in a context first of innocent love and then of love lost and doomed. Like Marie's memory of sledding in the mountains, the narrator's memory of shared feeling ends in evasion and loss, a refusal of life. In the first two passages memory and desire are linked, and the mood of anguish and despair arises from a sense of loss. Possible life seems to remain in the past, a choice not made and now remembered in regret. In the present there are only uncertainty and fear.

The first two passages of "The Burial of the Dead" point to possible meanings and values perceived as lost. The second and third shift to images and scenes of desolation, a world without value. In the third passage the narrator reports the words of Madame Sosostris, a fortune-teller whose pack of Tarot cards offers another way of knowing, of understanding one's life. Several times in *The Waste Land* voices are invoked of prophets or quasi-divine figures. This passage has both, the supposedly prophetic voice of the fortune-teller who reads the meaning of the cards and the cards themselves, which reveal truth supernaturally. But as the "Son of Man" was denied power and speech, Madame Sosostris is presented as a fraud. Although she points to the characters in the world, she reveals nothing about them. She cannot find the Hanged Man and is forbidden to see what the merchant carries. Her limited function is to introduce the key characters of the poem, but she cannot speak from outside the conditions she describes to offer insight or a warning.

Nonetheless, the characters she introduces and the remarks she makes sustain the tone of fear and unease already created. The narrator describes her in satiric tones as a wise woman with wicked cards despite her "bad cold" and as afraid herself to bring the horoscope, yet she defines the scope of human character in the poem. The sailor portends death by water. The woman is surrounded by disturbing connotations: belladonna is both a beautiful woman and a deadly drug; "lady of situations" has a sound of enticement or entrapment; "Lady of the Rocks" may suggest mermaids who lure men to their death or the Mona Lisa, who sits among the rocks and smiles mysteriously and hauntingly.[21] In the manuscript "Death by Water" began with a long description of sailors lured to their death by mermaids singing, and although—like the image of the wheel—it was dropped from the published poem, the cards that introduce both remain. The man with three staves is not directly explained and remains enigmatic here. In the notes, however, Eliot identifies him with the Fisher King, a figure who is wounded or ill and waiting to be restored. The merchant carries forbidden knowledge, and the Hanged Man, whom Eliot's note identifies with both a pagan god and Jesus, is missing. Crowds of people walk in circles. Madame Sosostris portrays the people we will encounter as shady, damaged, players in an unexplained but ominous drama.

When she tells the narrator that the drowned Phoenician Sailor is his card, he thinks, parenthetically, of a line from *The Tempest* about transformation in death. Ariel sings to Ferdinand, who mourns his father's supposed death by drowning:

> Full fathom five thy father lies,
> Of his bones are coral made,
> Those are pearls that were his eyes.
> Nothing of him that doth fade
> But doth suffer a sea change
> Into something rich and strange.
> Sea nymphs hourly ring his knell.
> (1.2.397–403.)

The narrator's one response is to this image, and he recalls it later in the poem in other situations. The idea of transformation, central to his musings, becomes the primary focus of "What the Thunder Said." Here it provides the only contrast to Madame Sosostris's "wicked" cards. Like the song from Wagner, this music offers relief, a brief release from dark imaginings. In other sections songs are often transient moments of beauty or poignance in depressing situations, but this song offers only an image to cling to. The passage closes with Madame Sosostris self-protective and fearful.

Of the characters introduced by Madame Sosostris, the crowds of people appear first. In the last passage of "The Burial of the Dead" the location moves to city streets, and the narrator's fear is extended to a social condition. The final scene acts as a culmination and a definition: it places the narrator in a kind of Hell, which he sees as the human condition. The city is dark and filled with despair and guilt, an atmosphere intensified by references to Dante's *Inferno* and by the narrator's encounter with Stetson, a moment of recognition resembling Dante's meetings with sinners.

Despite the move to crowds and cities, the fourth passage focuses on the same questions and images as the others—the linking of life and death, the disturbance of memory, the fear of spring and renewal. It begins in a mood of despairing recognition:

> Unreal City,
> Under the brown fog of a winter dawn,
> A crowd flowed over London Bridge, so many,
> I had not thought death had undone so many.

Here the narrator, who has been preoccupied with his own experience of death, sees in the world around him the same separateness, sorrow, and hopelessness. The people all look directly before them; they sigh; they are "undone." But the first line suggests a more specific fear. Eliot refers us to lines from Baudelaire: "Fourmillante cité, cité pleine de rêves, / Où le spectre en plein jour raccroche le passant." (Crowded city, city full of dreams, / Where the spectre in broad daylight stops the passerby.) To be haunted by ghosts, unable to forget the past, is the problem throughout "The Burial of the Dead," where roots will not lie quiescent but bloom and hurt, and memories remind one of present emptiness.

This opening image is expanded and intensified by other allusions, especially to Dante. The notes point to two references, the first to Dante's description of the souls in the vestibule of Hell who in life chose neither good nor evil and so go neither to Heaven nor to Hell. The lines, from *Inferno,* 3.55–57, express Dante's surprise at how many there are: "si lunga tratta / di gente, ch'io non avrei mai creduto / che morte tanta n'avesse disfatta" (such a long stream of people, that I should never have believed that death had undone so many). Their fate is, in one sense, the most terrible, for they have not lived at all. The second reference is from Dante's description of Limbo, inhabited by the souls who were virtuous on earth but unbaptized. They do not suffer but can never see God, and their sighs disturb the eternal air. Eliot picks up the "sighs" for his city crowds. As they walk the early, foggy streets, the church bells of Saint Mary Woolnoth chime the hour of nine—when city workers' hours began. The narrator hears it as a "dead" sound. Thus the one sound that claims to represent an authentic divine voice is again disclaimed. The concluding scene of the first section is a composite of quotations and references depicting impersonal masses swarming through streets oppressed by death and unrelieved by memory or religious promise. Memories are spectres, and the bells, like the prophets, lack an alternative message. We are left in a world where the promise of human love is a momentary dream succeeded by loss and regret, and where the promise of a meaning transcending the human appears only as fraud.

Within this context, the narrator suddenly becomes abrasive, urgent, accusing. He seems to know a deeper fear of hidden evil. His meeting with Stetson evokes a different kind of feeling, one that seems to draw on a more than personal memory. The battle of Mylae took place in the first Punic war (a trade war) in 260 B.C., yet he claims to have been there with Stetson. In one sense it suggests that all wars are the same. In another it emphasizes the narrator's reaction to the crowds, his sense that everyone is, like himself, alone and involved in a world of death. He consistently conflates contemporary and historic voices in his own, generalizing his experience and its origins in past failure.

Having identified Stetson with a historic past of fighting for trade, he brings him back to the present with the mysterious accusation of having "planted" a corpse in his garden. Is he implying a murder? a normal death? a metaphor for memories suppressed? the potential for life to emerge from death as in religious tradition? The text does not say. What is clear is that the narrator recalls the act with intense fear and dreads the consequences. He asks if something will grow and bloom from it, but he has already expressed anxiety at breeding flowers. And he fears that the frost has disturbed it or the dog will dig it up. Whatever it is, he wants it to stay hidden and is filled with horror at the thought that it may come to light.

"The Burial of the Dead"

If we think of the last passage separately, it reads as the agitated thoughts of one obsessed with an unnamed guilt and trapped in Hell. The landscape is nightmarish—foggy, dark, filled with the sound of sighs and the faces of strangers who seem familiar and anguished. When we read it in connection with the rest of the first section, it draws together images from the entire sequence into a culminating vision of life as deathlike, memory as a fearful past, and gardens and spring as the revelation of horror, not beauty. The earth, which in the opening offered an ambiguous rebirth, is now the uncertain container of a corpse. The final line makes a statement about what has been presented and functions as a prelude to the rest of *The Waste Land*. Not only the crowds of London are trapped in this Hell; like Stetson, the narrator insists, we are all in complicity. He speaks directly to the reader—again in the words of Baudelaire—and asserts our identity with him. Thus the narrator's meditations on a private inner experience open up into a claim of universal death and loss that no other voice counters. Neither prophets nor gods intervene, and their voices, when heard, prove false. In the following sections of the poem Eliot presents other characters of the waste land, observed and commented on by the narrator. They appear as successive demonstrations of the dark, encompassing vision of "The Burial of the Dead."

7

"A Game of Chess"

"A Game of Chess" differs in both structure and voice from "The Burial of the Dead." On an initial reading, it seems to be a quite separate poem, complete in itself and unconnected to what precedes it. There is not, in fact, any direct transition between them. Rather, the second poem begins in a new setting and introduces new voices. It consists of two scenes presented directly and dramatically. The two sets of characters are distinct and the situations initially quite different: the first takes place in the dressing room of an upper-class woman, the second in a working-class pub. Yet together they embody the despairing vision first defined in "The Burial of the Dead," a world devoid of human relationship or love. Both scenes portray contemporary events already cut off from any promise of the past. Unlike the narrator of the first section, these characters are preoccupied less with loss and regret than with the anxious present in which no sense of possibility or hope exists. They are trapped in self and in loveless marriages.

Their isolation and confinement take different forms, at least partly determined by class. In the first scene the couple are closed in a lavish dressing room, their tension hidden from others as they sit across a chessboard. If they go out, it is in a closed car. The lives of the second couple are public gossip, their most private fears and troubles exposed to all. Yet their sense of desperation is the same. The upper-class woman threatens to walk the streets; Lil insists that she can't help her looks. The juxtaposition of classes thus acts as an extension of personal experience into all of society. Surface differences mask a universal failure. For in both cases, the couples cannot speak to each other. They are totally cut off from each other and mutually alone. For Lil and Albert, sex is disconnected from either love or children; for the upper-class couple, no contact at all seems to occur.

With the shift to dramatic presentation, the poem shifts also from a private, meditative voice. It opens with a third-person description and moves to direct dialogue. The "I" of the first section has receded, and other figures move to the center—the tense and neurotic woman who urgently demands a response, Lil's acquaintance who tells the story of Lil and Albert's problems. The effect is to make more general and objective the narrator's sense of life and experience. Yet the narrator is not absent; he appears as the husband in the first scene and thus directly links the two poems. The identity of the narrator and the husband is made explicit both in images and in the notes. The husband says at one point, "I remember / Those are pearls that were his eyes," the line earlier quoted by the narrator. And in the note to that line, Eliot refers us to "Part I, 1. 37, 48."[22] Line 48 is "Those are pearls that were his eyes. Look!" But Line 37 seems puzzling at first. It is the reference to the Hyacinth garden. If we examine the facsimile edition, however, we see that the husband in "A Game of Chess" originally said, "I remember / the hyacinth garden. Those are pearls that were his eyes, yes." Eliot removed the first part of the line but did not correct the note. What is clear, however, is that the husband is the one who remembers the Hyacinth garden.

The narrator of section 1 has entered into a larger context rather than focusing on his private feelings. He is now a player in a larger drama than his own, and the experience of others dominates the poem. Nonetheless, his way of viewing life prevails. He describes the first scene, setting up our perception of the woman in advance. And though he is absent from the second scene, we read that in light of the first. We remain in a world seen through a central point of view even as we recognize many characters in it.

Like "The Burial of the Dead," "A Game of Chess" draws on material from Eliot's own life. Eliot's wife, Vivienne, wrote in the margin of the first scene, "WONDERFUL yes & wonderful wonderful," and Pound wrote at two points, "Photography?" and "photo," implying, according to Valerie Eliot's notes, "too realistic a reproduction of an actual conversation."[23] The pub scene was recounted to the Eliots by Ellen Kellond, a maid who worked for them. In both cases, however, the situations and characters are distanced and dramatized, and the poetic voice is less personal despite the use of personal sources. But "A Game of Chess," though it moves us out of private meditation into drama, sustains the themes introduced in "The Burial of the Dead." It presents specific illustrations of the lives of those living dead who walk London's streets and depicts their lonely isolation from one another.

Both the original title and the one Eliot chose suggest the meaning of these juxtaposed scenes. The first title was "In the Cage," a phrase immediately suggesting isolation, confinement, and entrapment. Recalling the epigraph from Petronius, it evokes both the Sibyl's cage and her longing for death because life is empty and without hope. Unlike the later title, moreover, it suggests the dominant image of air and death in air, hanging helplessly in nothingness. Critics have pointed out other sources for this title which are also suggestive in other ways. Henry James wrote a story entitled "In the Cage," in which a young woman who works as a telegrapher watches the lives of the rich through the telegrams they send. She works in a wire enclosure through which telegrams are thrust all day and imagines the lives of those she serves as filled with a grandness and complexity unattainable in her own dreary world and her engagement to a drab and methodical young man. She becomes absorbed in a love affair between an attractive man and a married woman, sending their private messages and arrangements for meetings back and forth. In the end, their affair turns out as unloving and sordid as her own. Like "A Game of Chess," the story contrasts upper- and lower-class love and finds them equally unreal, and the young woman's cage symbolizes her own sense of being cut off from any more significant world. A second possible source is a story by Virginia Woolf entitled "An Unwritten Novel," which Eliot had read. It contains the lines "The eyes of others our prisons, their thoughts our cages. Air above, air below."[24] The major character is a woman whom the narrator imagines as the protagonist of a novel and invests with a life story centered on a sense of hidden sin and guilt. Like Eliot's epigraph, it suggests directly the feeling of imprisonment and specifically the prison of other people's definitions.

The title Eliot chose is less obvious in its significance. There is a play by Thomas Middleton entitled *A Game of Chess*, but Eliot's notes refer to an actual game played in another Middleton play, *Women Beware Women*. The game is used to distract a mother-in-law's attention during the seduction of her daughter-in-law Bianca. The allusion focuses on deception and sexual violence, themes picked up in the images of Philomela and Albert's adulterous opportunities. But a more illuminating source of the title is a line in the original manuscript of the poem that Eliot removed at Vivienne's request. After line 137, "And we shall play a game of chess," the original version had the following line: "The ivory men make company between us." It makes clear the purpose of the game, to create an illusion of connection or relationship. If one plays a game, one need not talk. In "The Death of the Duchess," the earlier version of this scene omitted from the final poem, the significance of the situation is made explicit. The narrator, thinking of their inability to speak or understand each other, says, "If it is terrible alone, it is sordid with one more." Thus both titles point to the same terrible solitude of the ostensible lovers who are alone together.

Both the theme and the bitter mood of "A Game of Chess" are introduced by the opening lines, which allude to Shakespeare's *Antony and Cleopatra*:

> The Chair she sat in, like a burnished throne,
> Glowed on the marble, where the glass

Held up by standards wrought with fruited vines
From which a golden Cupidon peeped out
(Another hid his eyes behind his wing)

The notes point out the reference to Enobarbus's description of Cleo-patra's barge: "The barge she sat in, like a burnished throne, / Burned on the water. The poop was beaten gold, / Purple the sails. . . ." Eliot picks up both the rhythm and the lavish diction. More important, the scene suggests both love and betrayal. Enobarbus recalls the lovers' first meeting just after Antony has chosen to marry another woman—Caesar's sister Octavia—for political reasons. In Eliot's poem the ref-erence both establishes the subject of love and undercuts it; the barge is now only a chair before a dressing table, and the details are over-done and vulgar. The burnished throne quickly gives way to synthetic perfume, smoke, and cosmetic jars. What we find initially in this scene is both luxury and decadence, wealth and bad taste. Everything is overelaborate and overdone.

The entire opening description is heavy, opulent, a little nauseat-ing. Everything glitters, smells, shines, has intense colors: green, gold, orange. The diction is overly fine, full of words like *cupidon, profu-sion, unguent, laquearia,* and *sylvan.* The weight of the passage comes from this diction and the strong sensual images—thick air, smoke, odours, strange perfumes, over-full space. The atmosphere is stifling, and although nothing happens in the opening description until the last lines where footsteps shuffle and the woman brushes her hair, we are set up for themes of sex and betrayal by the lush scene and the allusions.

In the notes Eliot points to other sources besides *Antony and Cleopatra,* all of which have to do with similar themes. *Laquearia* is a Latin word meaning a paneled ceiling done in fretwork or decorative patterns. It is taken from a scene in Virgil's *Aeneid* where Dido gives a magnificent banquet for Aeneas, whom she loves and who later be-trays her. The language describing the banquet is, like that of Enobar-bus describing Cleopatra, lush and sensual. The "sylvan scene," Eliot notes, comes from Milton's *Paradise Lost.* Satan has just entered Paradise for the first time and sees before him a landscape of natural beauty—great trees laden with blossoms and fruit, sweet smells, pure air and gentle winds—all of which Adam and Eve enjoy and Satan will corrupt. It is the home of perfect love and harmony and will become the location of betrayal and sin. Eliot links it with the story of Philomela, portrayed on a painting above the mantelpiece in the dressing room. The story of Philomela is told in Ovid's *Metamorphoses*. Tereus married Procne and they had a son, Itys. Missing her sister, Philomela, Procne begged that she be brought to visit. To please her, Tereus returned to her home and brought back Philomela, but as soon as he saw her, he desired her. He raped her violently, and when she threatened to tell, cut out her tongue. But she wove a tapestry telling the tale and sent it to Procne, who avenged her sister by killing Itys and giving him to Tereus for dinner. When, in rage, he threatened revenge, the sisters escaped by turning into birds, Philomela into a nightingale and Procne into a swallow. The tale is bloody and violent, depicting not the betrayal of love but the brutal acting out of lust and violation. Yet it begins also in celebration of marriage and birth and later dwells on the beauty and rich appearance of Philomela.

If the foreground of the opening description is a silent dressing room where a tense woman merely brushes her hair, the background, repeatedly evoked by allusion, is sexual, violent, deceptive, and tragic. The description closes with an ominous image:

> Under the firelight, under the brush, her hair
> Spread out in fiery points
> Glowed into words, then would be savagely still.

She is taut, intense, disturbed. And as the description gives way to dialogue, her words reveal the situation. Her voice is consistently nervous and insistent, while the responses of the narrator are flat, distracted, and enigmatic. As she asks him repeatedly to speak with her, to tell her his thoughts, he offers disconnected remarks about dead men and remembers the line "Those are pearls that were his eyes." The bones and pearls recall the buried corpse and the warning of

Madame Sosostris; they do not answer her questions. The voices of the couple interact but do not connect: she demands; he remains withdrawn and separate. In one sense, this is a replaying of the Hyacinth garden scene without the veil of innocence and wistful desire. In both scenes a woman makes a claim to affection, communication, or response, and in both the narrator fails. The neurotic woman's accusations evoke his earlier thoughts: "Do / You know nothing? Do you see nothing? Do you remember / Nothing?" He remembers only the pearls, and, in the original manuscript, he remembered the Hyacinth garden where he "could not / Speak, and [his] eyes failed," and he "knew nothing, / Looking into the heart of light, the silence."

The drama of their mutual tension and isolation is played out without change or resolution. As she becomes more frantic, he thinks of light, frivolous dance music—the "Shakespearean Rag" was an actual song to which Eliot added the syncopation of "Shakespeherian"—and remains unable even to acknowledge her words. Her reaction is disturbing. She threatens to rush out and walk the streets with her hair down, like a prostitute, as if that is the one way left to gain attention. "What will we ever do?" she asks, and he lists the futile items of a daily routine: hot water, a closed car, a game of chess. They remain enclosed in the room, the car, the game, a cage for which rushing into the streets is no exit. The last line, alluding to the game of chess in *Women Beware Women*, links chess and seduction, reasserting the persistent background of sexual betrayal.

Like the first section, the second dramatizes parallel miseries without communication or sympathy. The scene is not described but pointed to by the reiterated call of the barman, "HURRY UP PLEASE IT'S TIME." It is a working-class pub at closing time. The voice this time belongs to an unnamed woman who gossips to an acquaintance about a couple they both know. In the background is the war from which Albert has just come home, wanting a good time. If the theme is again the failure of a couple to love or speak to each other, it takes the cruder form of overt sexual violation. The background of rape, deception, and violence is moved to the fore as the sordid conditions of Lil and Albert's relations. Lil is in bad health and has lost her looks bearing Albert's children. Her reward is to be blamed for no longer being sexually desirable. She has recently spent the money he gave her for new teeth to have an abortion, which damaged her more. Albert has come back brutalized by the war and feeling a right to some release and pleasure. The speaker sees it as an opportunity for herself to feel superior and gossip and, Lil suggests, to have her own affair with Albert. Her view is that Lil deserves to lose Albert for having her body ruined in his service. None of them imagines another life or a solution; they are as trapped as the first couple, all with needs and loneliness, all without speech to express their despair. Their reactions take the form of silence and desperate action: Lil takes pills for an abortion; Albert has affairs.

Like the first scene, the second ends in an allusion to betrayal. The pub is closing and the characters leaving, and the goodbyes are framed in the words of Ophelia's mad song in *Hamlet*. Driven mad by her father's murder and Hamlet's rejection, she says farewell to Hamlet's mother in these words and drowns herself: "Good night, ladies, good night, sweet ladies, good night, good night." This time it is a betrayal that kills. Thus "A Game of Chess," like "The Burial of the Dead," ends in an image of death. The first image was of a corpse in earth, and although Ophelia's death is by water, it is madness that really kills her. Madness is itself a kind of death; Ophelia's brother Laertes makes the connection when he wonders if "a young maid's wits / Should be as mortal as an old man's life." It is a kind of death by air, that is, the insubstantiality of madness, mere words and images in the air, a nothingness like the "nothing" in the narrator's head.

The image of air, in fact, though it does not appear in the title, reinforces the mood and theme throughout "A Game of Chess." The opening description is filled with smoke and smells, making the air thick and sensual. Air from the window stirs the scents and candle flames, and the noise of the wind terrifies the woman who asks repeatedly what it is doing. Disembodied voices hang in the air—the nightingale's "Jug Jug" and the barman's cry. And madness and nothingness dominate the talk. The first woman is neurotic and terrified, and she wildly asks her husband if he is even alive, if there is nothing in his head. The pub scene ends in madness as a kind of death. In the original version Eliot included another line that linked air and death overtly. When asked what the wind was doing, the narrator first answered, "Carrying / Away the little light dead people." In both theme and imagery the first two sections link emotional isolation, death, and the physical world.

In itself, "A Game of Chess" is a graphic, dramatic portrayal of madness, solitude, and the degradation of emotional and sexual relationships. Although the first scene depicts only an overstrained, even panicky, interchange on whether a man and woman can talk together at all or communicate in any way, the allusions sustain a persistent undercurrent of violence and guilt. Antony and Cleopatra's illicit love, Aeneas's betrayal of Dido, the brutal rapes of Philomela and the daughter-in-law in *Women Beware Women*, the corruption of Paradise and sin of Adam and Eve are all evoked to play off against the modern desperate couple. The violence comes to the surface in the second scene, where Albert's demands override Lil's health and possibly even life: "(She's had five already, and nearly died of young George.) / . . . Well, if Albert won't leave you alone, there it is, I said, / What you get married for if you don't want children?" Nor can Lil escape complicity, for she has an abortion with illegal pills and deceives Albert about the money for teeth. The "lady of situations" appears in both scenes as victim and victimizer, violated and destructive.

Juxtaposed to "The Burial of the Dead," "A Game of Chess" takes on broader significance as part of a larger Hell and a link in a series of encounters with physical experience. The undefined and sinister guilt of the first section gives way to a focus on more specific failures and sins, and the memory of youthful potential and innocent longing gives way to a sordid and hopeless present. If the Hyacinth garden remains the one image of a positive, fulfilling human connection, it dissolves in the narrator's reenactment of sightless and mute nonresponse. Neither rain nor sunlight nor hyacinths appear, and past promise has already failed.

In "The Burial of the Dead" the alternative voices of prophecy speak, only to be dismissed. In "A Game of Chess" the only voices are those of the lost. The narrator no longer contemplates another answer to his questions, and the immediate voices of the woman and Lil's friend dominate. The voices from outside the situation that interweave with theirs are the cries of victims, Philomela and Ophelia. Interestingly, despite the greater futility and anguish of "A Game of Chess," we are likely to read it as less disturbing than the first section. Because the surface tone is ironic and the diction deliberately overworked in the opening description, and because the gossiping woman in the pub is almost comic in her phrasing and attitudes, the horror of what actually occurs is displaced. Rhythms reinforce this displacement. The first dialogue is quick and tense, the movement staccato. It is broken by the jazzy syncopation of "Shakespeherian Rag" and the slight lyric phrase "Those are pearls that were his eyes." Only in the narrator's brief responses do the earlier feelings of weariness and fear surface. Reading the second scene, we are even more distanced by the catty, gossiping voice and the rhythms of ordinary speech. The mutual sniping of the speaker and Lil lighten, even trivialize, what they discuss:

> He's been in the army four years, he wants a good time,
> And if you don't give it him, there's others will, I said.
> Oh is there, she said. Something o' that, I said.
> Then I'll know who to thank, she said, and give me a straight look.

The barman's interjected calls repeatedly break up the talk, reminding us that this is just chat in a pub at closing time and cutting off development of the disturbing theme. Without the narrator's interpretive commentary, these scenes appear at first almost as documentaries, slices of modern life characterized by tension and futility but unconnected to any deeper meaning. But the allusions and cross-references insist on placing them in a larger context.

In "The Burial of the Dead" the narrator's fear and despair are immediate and central. Here the sources of emotion are either beneath the surface or masked by comic simplicity. The effect is to sustain a separation between the unresolved and uncomprehended tensions of our surface lives and their more terrible depths.

Only in the most tenuous way does a hint of another world or life enter "A Game of Chess." The narrator still recalls the image of transformation, "Those are pearls that were his eyes." And Philomela, transformed into a nightingale, fills the desert with "inviolable" voice. Both images suggest a rebirth of beauty out of death. Yet even that is undercut in the case of Philomela, whose song is now heard by dirty ears as "Jug Jug," a phrase that, in Elizabethan poetry, meant both a bird's song and (crudely) sexual intercourse. Moreover, the narrator remembers the pearl image, ironically, at the moment when he again fails to speak or see another. It is as if whatever slight hint of positive values may appear is inapprehensible. Just as Madame Sosostris could not find the Hanged Man or see what the merchant carried, and the Son of Man could not say, the narrator is repeatedly said to be blind and without speech. He and, by extension, all the characters are alone and trapped in their solitude and guilt, cut off from any regenerative power. Thus "A Game of Chess," taken in relation to "The Burial of the Dead," moves further into the world of the narrator's deepest fears, a place where life itself is a kind of death like that of the Sibyl in the cage.

8

"The Fire Sermon"

Writing in 1932, F. R. Leavis called Eliot's note on Tiresias the "clue to *The Waste Land*." "It indicates plainly enough," he said, "what the poem is: an effort to focus an inclusive human consciousness."[25] The introduction of Tiresias, in other words, signifies that the poem presents not particular experience but the human experience. And in fact, "The Fire Sermon" serves, more than either of the first two sections, to generalize and extend the narrator's consciousness, not only by the introduction of Tiresias but by the broadening of content and addition of speakers. While "The Burial of the Dead" focuses on the narrator's private fears and experience, and "A Game of Chess" dramatizes specific events in the larger social world he envisages, "The Fire Sermon" interweaves scenes from modern London, the London of Queen Elizabeth I, and ancient Greece. It is longer and more varied than the previous sections, and its wide range of images and situations is presented as part of a single human condition. Both the structure—a series of many scenes in different styles—and the changing voices suggest this enlarging of definition. Yet despite Tiresias's claim to speak for all humanity, the central vision of "The Fire Sermon" remains that of the narrator; it is he who interprets and responds to his own experience and to the world portrayed by others.

"The Fire Sermon" is rich in voices and dense with allusion. Phrases and images from Spenser, Shakespeare, Marvell, Verlaine, Ovid, Sappho, Goldsmith, Wagner, Dante, Augustine, and Buddha are acknowledged in the notes along with popular songs, the nightingale, and the sounds of automobiles. Although the narrator speaks first and returns between other passages, the voices of Tiresias and the Thames-daughters are granted both space and authority. What they say, however, echoes and reinforces what the narrator has said. Tiresias claims to speak for both sexes, and the Thames-daughters echo that the world as women know it is the same. Tiresias claims to have foresuffered all, to have known it all in advance, and the Thames-daughters speak for Elizabeth I as well as themselves. She too has known what they know. Augustine and Buddha remind us that the fires of passion burn always. Each voice, whether contemporary and private or inclusive and prophetic, adds to an expanding vision of a world where sex is disconnected from love, commitment, or religious significance.

The narrator speaks first, in a new mood compounded of regret and sympathy. Removed from a dramatic context, he speaks again as both observer and participant, contemplating and lamenting human experience. He is less blank and restrained, and responds more emotionally to what he sees. He remembers songs of innocence—the refrain from *Prothalamion*, the "pleasant whining of a mandoline," and the voices of infants singing in a tower. He weeps. He cries out, "O City city." But his grief in the opening suddenly gives way to the fear and terror of death characteristic of "The Burial of the Dead," and his tone varies from sardonic remarks on Mrs. Porter to a flat report of Mr. Eugenides, to a reverence for the splendor of Magnus Martyr. In "The Fire Sermon" the narrator's emotional responses include more kinds of feeling and suggest more ways of reacting to the world than horror or withdrawal. His thoughts are linked to those of his earlier appearances by recurring images of rats, hidden bones, death by water, and Philomela. But these reminders of death, guilt, and violation are juxtaposed to images of marriage and singing children and fishmen lounging in a bar. If the world he observes remains sordid, the possibility of another world is more present.

At the center of "The Fire Sermon" and the center of the entire poem, Tiresias speaks. Like the Son of Man and Madame Sosostris, he speaks with the gift of prophecy. But his speech is neither denied nor ironically dismissed. Rather, he is granted, in the notes, the encompassing vision of the whole poem. What he sees, we are told, is its substance. The relationship between the narrator and Tiresias is more complex than between the narrator and other characters with whom he speaks, such as Stetson or even Madame Sosostris. As one commentator points out:

> We have to distinguish the scenes in which the protagonist himself plays a part—the recollection of the Hyacinth garden, the visit to Madame Sosostris, the meeting with Stetson, the scene with the rich Belladonna—from the scenes in the pub and at the typist's. We can either consider that the protagonist overhears the first and imagines the second, or that at these points the poet's consciousness takes leave of the protagonist to portray parallel instances.[26]

He preferred, he added, the first line of interpretation, and I agree. The poem is more comprehensible and rich if we recognize and account for the narrator's persistent presence, recurrent allusions and memories, and consistent themes. If we take Tiresias, then, as a figure imagined by the narrator, his focus on the unmeaning, casual, and automatic nature of sex generalizes the narrator's despair and emotional isolation to all humanity, past and present. Because Tiresias has been both man and woman, has been present since ancient times, and knows the future, he is presented as an inclusive, almost supernatural voice. Yet what he sees is not distinct from what the narrator sees. Though he provides an apparently objective survey of experience, he does not represent another point of view, nor does he offer any solution or answer to the questions posed by this vision.

The Thames-daughters also speak in "The Fire Sermon." Their "song" is in two stanzas, juxtaposing, like the narrator's opening scene, Elizabethan and modern London. They then speak in succession of seduction and despair. Like the narrator, they remain passive and expect nothing. The women in all of "The Fire Sermon" engage briefly and automatically in sex without the desire of the hyacinth girl or the hysteria and desperation of those in "A Game of Chess." Thus the voices of women, too, reiterate what the narrator fears and Tiresias "sees." Like Philomela, they are raped, but unlike her, they seem neither to feel rage nor to desire revenge. They express only a futile and quiet despair: "What should I resent?" "I can connect / Nothing with nothing."

The stories of the narrator, Tiresias, and the Thames-daughters all focus on the theme announced by the title, the fires of passion and lust. But this is called a "sermon," a warning as well as a description. It ends with phrases from St. Augustine and Buddha in what Eliot calls the "collocation of these two representatives of eastern and western asceticism."[27] Both Buddha and Augustine speak from outside ordinary experience of the need to suppress desire and achieve a higher state of existence. For the first time, here, voices representing religious truth offer answers, identifying passion and lust as the source of anguish and despair.

Thus while the "substance of the poem" seems in one sense to become more terrible, as Tiresias universalizes the narrator's condition, in another sense it becomes less so. Although it expands to include all people, it also includes other moods, responses, and possibilities. Traces of another kind of experience appear in the images of innocence or sacredness, the ability to weep, and the call for asceticism. They remain, however, only traces, emerging briefly to be replaced with remembered fear and sordid encounters.

The narrator's altered mood appears in the opening passage, a sustained contrast between the Thames as bearer of flower-strewn and lovely brides and as location of brief liaisons. We are returned to the landscape as symbol of death and loss. It is late autumn or winter, and both life and love recede:

> The river's tent is broken: the last fingers of leaf
> Clutch and sink into the wet bank. The wind
> Crosses the brown land, unheard. The nymphs are departed.

The image is of the branches, which in summer meet over the water and form a tent, losing their leaves and ceasing to form a protective canopy. But it changes quickly to an image of drowning as the leaves, like fingers, clutch the bank and are pulled down.

This is again a dead land, but it was once living. In Spenser's *Prothalamion,* from which the refrain, "Sweet Thames, run softly till I end my song," is taken, Spenser walks along the river to ease his "sullein care" and sees young women—"a flock of nymphs"—gathering flowers to toss on a boat carrying two brides. *Prothalamion* (the title means "before the bridal chamber") is a poem in celebration of marriage and the ability of love to displace darker feelings. Eliot's allusion to Spenser is partly ironic; it reveals, by contrast, the degradation of modern sex enacted among sandwich papers, cigarette ends, and empty bottles rather than garlands of flowers and sweet songs. But it is also a memory invoked to affirm another way of experiencing the world.

The allusion to *Prothalamion* is linked, moreover, with a biblical allusion to the sorrow of the Israelites while captive in Babylon. "By the waters of Leman I sat down and wept . . ." recalls "By the rivers of Babylon, there we sat down, yea, we wept, when we remembered Zion." The desolation of exile is intensified in this instance by the wordplay on "Leman." Lake Leman is the French name for Lake Geneva in Switzerland, where Eliot, in his own emotional and physical exile, wrote the poem. "Leman" also means a lover, and the connotations are ambiguous. It can mean a sweetheart and occasionally a husband or wife. It is even used at times in reference to Christ or the Virgin as the beloved. But it can also mean a mistress or prostitute. It combines the ideas of illicit sensuality and true or sacred love. The context does not distinguish here, and the line becomes a lamentation over love itself, whether the anguish of transient passion or separation from genuine relation. If Spenser's refrain points to the latter, the sudden memory of bones and cold wind insist on the former.

The remembered cold wind and rattle of bones, too, have a double suggestiveness, for while the images are drawn from the earlier thoughts of chill and death, the phrasing of the following lines ("But at my back from time to time I hear") comes from Marvell's "To His Coy Mistress," a poem of seduction. In this opening scene of "The Fire

Sermon" moods and meanings shift and change, and the narrator's ambivalent stance reminds us of the initial question: "What are the roots that clutch, what branches grow / Out of this stony rubbish?" The question had seemed closed in the face of either terror and guilt or blank withdrawal, but in this loosening of grief and tears, it comes to the fore.

In the second passage the narrator is identified with Ferdinand and with the Fisher King of Jessie Weston. Eliot comments in the note on Tiresias that these characters are not wholly distinct; in this scene all three appear as the narrator fishes and recalls his father's wreck. According to Weston, the Fisher King is sometimes depicted as a character who fishes. Madame Sosostris's cards introduced the man with three staves whom Eliot associates "quite arbitrarily, with the Fisher King himself," and who appears for the first time here.[28] By identifying with this mythic figure, whose wound or illness is linked to the death of the land, the narrator expresses a sense of guilt and need for restoration, and makes himself an archetypal figure whose sickness pervades human society.

The narrator is identified also with Ferdinand, who recalls his father's death and is comforted by Ariel's music and the image of pearls. In *The Tempest* he meets and loves Miranda, his father is discovered to be alive, and his wedding is promised. But he is also the modern man who remains haunted by thoughts of hidden bones and bodies. The "White bodies naked on the low damp ground" are linked with images of death and with the bodies of lovers on the riverbank. Thus the narrator is both the wounded or dying king and the son/ lover who imagines a transforming death, as he will also be the drowned sailor and the merchant. What these roles have in common are love and death in their contrasting forms of fulfillment and destruction. In the land laid waste by the Fisher King's wound or illness, life is not renewed and women do not give birth, but with his cure generation will be restored. Ferdinand muses on both death and bodies, but in *The Tempest* he regains his father and is betrothed to Miranda.

The complicated conjunctions of this passage continue with references to Sweeney and Mrs. Porter and the infants in the tower. Three images come together in the Sweeney lines: a music-hall song, the character of Sweeney who, in earlier Eliot poems, is a crude vulgarian, and the story of Actaeon and Diana. The huntsman Actaeon came upon Diana (goddess of chastity) bathing with her nymphs and, in punishment for looking upon her naked, was turned into a stag and torn to death by hounds. Whatever goes on between Sweeney and Mrs. Porter carries no such significance and has no tragic consequences; the image of violation as a great evil is reduced to a cheap affair. In line 202 voices of innocent children form a contrast to both. This line, from Verlaine's *Parsifal*, describes children singing at a ceremony preceding the Fisher King's restoration.

In this complex passage Eliot uses a dense mass of allusion to evoke varying images of death and rebirth. The narrator is thoughtful, repelled, satiric, and longing by turns as he takes on different characters and imagines death and love in different forms. If we take these allusions as scraps of phrases and images in the narrator's mind, they expand and vary his own immediate response to the London scene with a long history of human experience. His feelings of regret, longing, fear, and revulsion are intensified by the parallel or contrasting stories of love and death. In another sense, he incorporates them, making his own response universal.

The following sections return to earlier images that are part of the narrator's personal memory: the song of Philomela, associated with the dialogue in "A Game of Chess," and the "Unreal City" of "The Burial of the Dead." These earlier references appear in the context of the narrator's more ambivalent mood and become even harsher by contrast. The "Unreal City," for example, is the setting for another kind of brief liaison. The Metropole is a fashionable hotel at Brighton on the southern coast of England. Because a "weekend at Brighton" is a phrase understood to carry sexual connotations, this scene has been taken to depict a homosexual proposition. Although the event actually occurred to Eliot, who denied thinking of that implication, it is difficult to see its function in the poem otherwise. As a suggestion to engage in a casual and unfruitful sexual act, it has emotional links with all the contacts Eliot presents as automatic and unfeeling.

The first four passages of "The Fire Sermon" form a set in which the narrator's thoughts shift and change, linking the scene on the banks of the Thames, his earlier fear of the dead land, his horror of sexuality and death, and his longing for genuine human communication and relation first portrayed in the talk with Marie and the Hyacinth garden. As he takes on the different personalities of the Fisher King and Ferdinand, the same concerns present themselves in different forms and alter their significance. It is as if he were exploring the many ways in which one can approach or consider human fate.

With the shift to the voice of Tiresias, the extension of experience is total. And yet there is a certain irony in the fact that the prophetic vision of one who encompasses all human experience narrows to so particular and limited an event as the seduction of a typist by a clerk. The melodramatic horror of Philomela's rape and mutilation and the tragic effects of the Fisher King's wound are displaced by the petty vanity of a "low" young man and the bored acquiescence of a woman unburdened by consciousness. If Tiresias insists that what he sees is what he himself has known throughout history, it is also a projection of the narrator's deepest terror, that the link of men and women is simply nothing at all. Embedded in a mosaic of scenes in which sex is violent, tragic, magnificent, or poignant, the voice of Tiresias reasserts the narrator's own inability to respond with any emotion, either positive or negative. Tiresias, while in one sense all-inclusive, is, in another sense, exclusive: he "sees" sexuality only in its lowest form and offers that as emblematic.

The typist's scene is placed between two images of human desire as mechanical and unmeaning. It opens with the dehumanized urgency of a "human engine . . . / Like a taxi throbbing waiting" and closes with an "automatic hand" that "puts a record on the gramophone." The language, for the most part, is realistic and crude, though traces of opposing feeling appear as usual in brief allusions and intensify the scene by contrast. Tiresias tells us that he is an old man with "wrinkled female breasts" and repeats that he has "wrinkled dugs." He emphasizes ugliness with such terms and with harshly satirical comments on the "low" class of both characters, the typist's "food in tins" and "drying combinations," the clerk's pimples and "bold stare" and "assurance." Tiresias's tone is contemptuous and judgmental. The crudeness of what he sees is emphasized by the contrasting mood of "the evening hour that strives / Homeward, and brings the sailor home from sea," a phrase from a lyric prayer to the evening star by Sappho. The lines also recall the sailor of the first section who sings of home and his love. By this interweaving and reiteration Eliot sustains the memory of many ways of feeling that may reinforce or undercut the immediate one.

The most depressing quality of the typist episode is that it seems devoid of all emotion. The blank separation of the narrator from the hyacinth girl or the nervous woman of "A Game of Chess" evoked a claim to affection or hysterical demands, and caused him unease or despair. Here the physical act is carried out with no feeling except lust and boredom. The language of violence is used ("assaults," "no defense"), but the act is unresisted and unresented. She is left untouched, as if nothing had occurred, and he leaves without minding. Sex is not a profound act of moral significance but an animal coupling devoid of intimacy or significance in past or future. We all seek in sex an affirmation of connection with another, an assurance that the other is moved by us, a sense of giving ourselves and receiving the other. The typist and clerk give and receive nothing; they engage in the most total contact available to humans and leave each other wholly alone. If there is a deeper terror than violation and death, it is utter solitude. That the typist and clerk are unconscious of their fate intensifies its significance for Tiresias, who juxtaposes the clerk's indifference to his own experience of human tragedy and Hell:

> (And I Tiresias have foresuffered all
> Enacted on this same divan or bed;
> I who have sat by Thebes below the wall
> And walked among the lowest of the dead.)

In Sophocles' *Oedipus Tyrannus*, when Thebes is laid waste by the sin of Oedipus, Tiresias knows and reveals the cause of the curse. In Homer's *Odyssey* Tiresias appears in Hell. He has seen both a destroyed and infertile land, like that of the Fisher King, and souls in Hell, like those of Dante and the London crowds. He places this loveless encounter in the context of such human failure and despair. The point is pressed again by allusion to an alternative response. Eliot closes the scene with a reference to Goldsmith's *The Vicar of Wakefield* in which a young woman who was seduced sings a song of grief and regret:

> When lovely woman stoops to folly,
> And finds too late that men betray,
> What charm can sooth her melancholy
> What art can wash her guilt away?
> The only art her guilt to cover,
> To hide her shame from every eye,
> To give repentance to her lover,
> And wring his bosom—is to die.

The contrasting allusions set up an opposition between sex as a moral act for good or evil and sex as empty gesture, the burning of passion divorced from value. The latter is linked to the most terrible and destructive symbols of the human condition: the ruined, infertile land and the realm of the dead.

Although Tiresias speaks only once in *The Waste Land*, his vision is granted authority by its central placement and by Eliot's explanatory note. Yet his vision is also limiting and limited. He precludes the many changing ways of interpreting experience expressed by the narrator in his many guises. And he "sees," in fact, only the outward act and interprets the attitude; he does not speak *for* the characters. The Thames-daughters speak for the typist more than he, and their sad songs evoke pity more than contempt. In the distanced and objective voice of Tiresias, Eliot was able to express revulsion directly and even abrasively. But when his characters speak for themselves, they reveal a more complex human lot. In an early poem, "Preludes," Eliot follows a series of portraits of sordid figures with lines more apt for many of those trapped in the waste land than Tiresias's world-weary dismissal:

"The Fire Sermon"

> I am moved by fancies that are curled
> Around these images, and cling:
> The notion of some infinitely gentle
> Infinitely suffering thing.

It is not that such feelings are removed from *The Waste Land* but that they are absent from Tiresias, who claims to speak from outside the situation and with inclusive vision. Thus the prophetic voice, when it appears with acknowledged authority, seems oddly detached from the wider knowledge of the poem.

The reappearance of the narrator abruptly shifts the tone. Ariel's music brings back the scene of Ferdinand musing on his father's death, carrying with it all the significance of transforming death, restoration, and young love. And the modern voice immediately recurs with a moving recollection of momentary beauty even in London, of mandolin music, fishmen enjoying themselves at lunch in a bar, and the white and gold of Magnus Martyr. This passage is perhaps the most positive and accepting in the entire poem. Ariel's song and the mandolin are harbingers of renewal and ease, and the "inexplicable splendour" of Magnus Martyr seems to transcend physical beauty.

This passage is interesting also for its portrayal of the fishmen at ease. While allusions to literature and the past import into the poem images of kings, queens, and princes whose lives are heroic or tragic or capable of desire, the working class of London have been portrayed in uniformly negative ways. The crowds in the streets are undone; Lil and Albert are both comic and sordid; the nymphs and loitering heirs are unappealing; and the typist and clerk are almost offensive. Only these fishmen—workers from a nearby fish market—and the drowned sailor are exempt from such connotations. In both cases, they seem to exist apart from the general world of sin and decay.

The compelling innocence of fishmen's chatter and Ionian white and gold gives way to a two-stanza lyric still set on the Thames. In the notes Eliot calls it the "Song of the (three) Thames-daughters." They are working-class young women who, like the others of "The Fire Sermon," are seduced and betrayed, but who tell their own stories and

set them in the ironic context of the changing river and changing be-
havior. Their song juxtaposes the Thames as it appears in modern
London and as it appeared to Elizabeth I.

The first stanza presents an ugly and degraded image of the river,
its tone created by harsh diction and allusion. The red sails and barges
drifting with the tide are drawn from the opening of Conrad's *Heart
of Darkness*, from which the original epigraph was taken. For Conrad,
the Thames led into an immeasurable darkness, and the song evokes
again the horror of Kurtz's self-realization. It seems likely that Eliot
also had in mind scenes from *Our Mutual Friend*, from which the
original title was taken. Much of the novel takes place on or beside
the Thames, which Dickens describes as filthy and filled with coal
barges and slime, and which repeatedly turns up the bodies of
drowned men. The sounds are crude and heavy: "sweats / Oil and tar,"
"swing on the heavy spar," "the Isle of Dogs." It is a setting only;
nothing takes place except the turning of the tide and the drifting of
logs. But it establishes an attitude toward the river and those who sail
on it that is appropriately closed with a lament: "Weialala leia / Wal-
lala leialala." The grieving song is taken from the song of the Rhine
maidens who, in Wagner's *Götterdämmerung* (*Twilight of the Gods*),
weep because the river's gold has been stolen and the river's beauty is
gone.

The second stanza creates, again through diction and allusion, a
starkly contrasted scene of courtly magnificence. The boat is again a
royal barge, and the description recalls that of Cleopatra with its pur-
ple and gold. This time it is Elizabeth I and her courtier in a game of
flirtation, which Eliot describes in the notes. The words are chosen to
evoke beauty, richness, and purity—"gilded shell / Red and gold," a
rippling wind, bells, and white towers. Like many of Eliot's evocations
of a splendid past, this carries an ambiguous suggestion. In one sense
the scene is glorious and opposed to the sweating modern river with
its oil and tar and drifting logs. In another sense it is just the same, as
the loves of Elizabeth were transient, illicit, and unfulfilled. This scene
ends in the same lament for lost beauty despite its surface charm.

The song of the Thames-daughters creates a context for their personal stories. It sets up a background of loss and despair against which their voices become individualized examples of general sorrow. Their stories are all the same; they tell of their violation and speak of their emptiness and disconnection. They emphasize their location, as if it is key to their fate. The first is from Highbury, a residential district of London, but her seduction occurred in a riverside district, by Richmond. The second places her ruin in Moorgate, an area in the City of London near where Eliot worked at Lloyd's Bank. The third is at Margate, the seaside resort on the Thames estuary where Eliot began writing *The Waste Land*. Eliot places them all near London, in familiar places, and in two cases near the river. The third insists on her lower-class origins. They are thus all women like the typist. And they share her passivity and disconnection from either moral or emotional involvement in what is done to them.

The words they choose emphasize this passivity. The first speaks only of what has been done to her: "bore me," "undid me." She raises her knees and is "supine." The second makes no comment while her seducer weeps. She asks, "What should I resent?" The third parallels the narrator in her focus on "nothing," a word invoked in both the Hyacinth garden episode and the conversation with the nervous, demanding woman. Now it is the woman who feels nothing; the solitude and disconnection previously felt by the narrator become defining characteristics of women as well, and the typist's reaction extends to the rest. The concluding "la la" has an odd tone. It is again the Rhine maidens' lament and sustains the note of mourning. Yet by itself it has an almost casual, dismissive ring. Their poignant song is cut off, perhaps as an emblem of their emotional debility. The urgency of grief, too, declines. Yet the entire section of the Thames-daughters sets up a contrast to the scene of the typist. Unlike the typist and the clerk, these women recognize, despite their passivity, the fact of their loss. In fact, "The Fire Sermon" is filled with lamentation. The narrator weeps by the waters of Leman and cries "O City city." The Thames-daughters lament. The seducer weeps.

"The Fire Sermon," though it contains material as disturbing as that in either "The Burial of the Dead" or "A Game of Chess," ends differently. The first two sections end in the voices of angry accusation and madness. Death in earth, the corpse in the garden, evokes in the narrator a haunting guilt and insistence on our complicity. The mad voice of Ophelia, a kind of death in air, reiterates the hopeless imprisonment of all the characters in "A Game of Chess." But the fire at the end of "The Fire Sermon" is offered by the quasi-divine voices of religious teachers as an admonition and call for change. In both Buddha's "Fire Sermon" and Augustine's *Confessions* fire is identified with passion. And in both the only hope for spiritual perfection is renunciation of passion and freedom from desire.

According to Henry Clark Warren, whose translation of Buddhist texts Eliot refers to in the notes, "The term 'Buddha' means 'Enlightened one,' and signifies that the person to whom it is applied has solved the riddle of existence, and discovered the doctrine for the cessation of misery."[29] The central issues of *The Waste Land* might be called "the riddle of existence" and "the cessation of misery"; hence the Buddha's appearance at the close of "The Fire Sermon" comes as at least a possible answer to the question posed in the beginning. The placing together of the Buddha and St. Augustine not only reinforces that answer by repetition, it once again universalizes the conception by bringing together Eastern and Western thought. Augustine, moreover, speaks from a double perspective as one who in youth pursued pleasure and lived by desire but later renounced passion for a religious life.

"All things," says the Buddha in his Fire Sermon, "are on fire . . . with the fire of passion, . . . with the fire of hatred, with the fire of infatuation; with birth, old age, death, sorrow, lamentation, misery, grief, and despair are they on fire."[30] It is almost a description of *The Waste Land*. "The learned and noble disciple," claims the Buddha, conceives an aversion to all sensation and to the mind and ideas and mind-consciousness, and is then divested of passion and becomes free. St. Augustine could be said to have acted out this scenario. In *The Confessions* he describes his life in Carthage surrounded by a "cauldron of unholy loves."[31] He then describes his conversion and release from desire. Thus the allusions placed together at the end of "The Fire

Sermon" are very directly focused on "the substance of the poem," the misery and meaninglessness chronicled from the opening images of generation and death, memory and desire. Because fire is both the burning of passion and the purifying fire of purgation, one might take this either way or both ways. Regardless of the emphasis, the voices of Buddha and Augustine are presented as an authentic expression of higher wisdom, validated, like the voice of Tiresias, by Eliot's notes as well as by their juxtaposition to the laments of the victims of desire.

In "The Fire Sermon" the characters of *The Waste Land* are more various and more generalized while the narrator's mood is less constrained. As the narrator moves toward a release of emotion—sorrow and regret and yearning for another world—and the voices of women assume the form of lamentation, the voices of both secular knowledge and divine wisdom intervene to define the source of despair and offer a solution. This is not to say that asceticism is embraced either here or in the poem as a whole. Rather it is set up in opposition to the misery depicted over and over as the outcome of human involvement in physical existence.

9

"Death by Water"

The fourth section of *The Waste Land* differs strikingly from the first three. It is a single brief lyric, spoken by the narrator alone, and the tone is significantly altered. Perhaps the most striking change is its great calm and its distance from the sources of earlier feeling. It is not set in London but at sea. There are no women, only water and tides and currents. No passions intrude, neither the fires of desire nor the terror of generation and death. The narrator's tone is quiet, accepting, a little solemn, but it holds no horror.

This section is anticipated from the first words of Madame Sosostris, "Here . . . / Is your card, the drowned Phoenician Sailor," and the narrator's linking of the card with Ariel's song. Though Madame Sosostris warned the narrator to "fear" death by water, the Phlebas passage retains none of that feeling. The wheel forecast by Madame Sosostris makes its only appearance here. Her card had originally introduced the wheel of fortune Pound cut from "The Fire Sermon" ("London, your people is bound upon the wheel"), but here it is the steering wheel of a ship firmly gripped by sailors with "a concentrated will against the tempest and the tide."[32] Other images recur in this section—a dead body, bones, and the cry of birds. More generally, images of death and physical disintegration recur in quite different form. Each repeated image takes on a new quality in this context. The drowned sailor, identified in the opening with the narrator, is characterized not by "memory and desire" but by forgetting and peace. His image evokes neither fear nor unease; his body quietly rises and falls with the sea swell. The bones, which were lost in rats' alley and "cast in a little low dry garret, / Rattled by the rat's foot," are now picked "in whispers." The wheel, undefined in Madame Sosostris's speech, is an instrument of control held by all kinds of people. The series of images thus replaces passion with freedom from desire, memory with forgetting, a dry garret with vast seas, the rattling of rats' feet with whispering currents.

"Death by Water" works not by its statements, which are descriptive and enigmatic, but by its calming diction and imagery. It is hushed, released from the tension and terror of the human world of cities, noises, and sexuality. In Eliot's best-known earlier poem, "The Love Song of J. Alfred Prufrock," Prufrock imagines escaping from lonely city streets to the floor of the sea: "I should have been a pair of ragged claws / Scuttling across the floors of silent seas." "Prufrock" ends in an image of lingering in chambers of the sea, drawn there by the songs of sirens, and drowning when recalled by human voices. There, too, the depths of the sea appear as a separate physical world of release and rest. The drowned sailor seems to move further into that inhuman world as he passes "the stages of his age and youth / Entering the whirlpool."

The form of this section was not originally intended to be so distinctive. In the manuscript, it included three sections, the first a description of sailors and the second a long narrative of a shipwreck at sea, which contained all the fear and terror of earlier material. All but the brief lyric was cut by Pound. But it was clearly meant, even in the original context, to provide a contrast and relief from the preceding material. In the published poem it has the effect of lifting us out of the "burning" of passion with which "The Fire Sermon" closes. But even the passage about Phlebas itself had earlier forms suggesting quite different moods. "Dirge," another version probably written in 1921, is

crudely satiric and includes a sardonic contrast to Ariel's song about
pearls and transformation. In this form, the lyric focuses not on the
calm but on the physical horror of death. Still another earlier version,
untitled, dwells on physical decay but closes with the stillness and
quiet of death:

> Those are pearls that were his eyes. See!
> And the crab clambers through his stomach, the eel grows big
> And the torn algae drift above him,
> And the sea colander.
> Still and quiet brother are you still and quiet[33]

Both versions are included in the manuscript, but were cut from the
published poem. The version that was retained keeps the sense of quiet
and removes all concern with organic dissolution.

There is another, more interesting, earlier version. In 1920 Eliot
published a poem in French called "Dans le Restaurant." The lyric that
became section 4 of *The Waste Land* is simply a slightly revised trans-
lation of the final stanza. Eliot is again alluding to his own previous
work, but this time the source was published and available, inviting
comparison. In "Dans le Restaurant" the Phlebas passage follows,
rather abruptly, a scene in which an old waiter tells the story of his
initiation into sex at the age of seven. The speaker, a young man, is
angry and disgusted by the old man's unwanted confidences and by
his shabbiness and dirtiness. He calls the waiter an old lecher and tells
him to clean the dirt from his face. In the end he asks by what right
the old man has experiences like his and hands him money for a bath.
On the surface, the poem may seem to present an especially sordid
scene of "burning" from which Phlebas is released and cleansed by
drowning.

But the significance of this context becomes more clear if we ex-
amine the exact nature of the old waiter's story. It is, in fact, the mem-
ory of a moment of innocent, childhood joy, paralleling in many
details the episode in the Hyacinth garden. For though the young man
is revolted by his image of the waiter as a lewd and filthy old man,

the experience happened to a very young child playing with another. The old waiter begins by saying that in his country it is the rainy season, a time of wind, grand sunshine, and rain. "It is what we call the washing day of the beggars." He describes the rain-soaked willows where he took refuge from a shower. He remembers that he was seven. The little girl was even younger. She was all damp, and he gave her flowers and tickled her to make her laugh. "I experienced a moment of power and delirium." But a big dog came, and he was afraid. He stopped halfway. "It is a pity," he concludes, and the young man reacts with revulsion. But the memory, in itself, is poignant. As in the Hyacinth garden, the girl is wet with rain and he gives her flowers. Some moment of ecstasy occurs but is broken off. It is the likeness to his own experience that disturbs the young man.

"Dans le Restaurant" functions, like the other allusions, to bring into *The Waste Land* a larger range of significance. Section 4 carries the resonance of the scene between the young man and the old waiter, reminding us again of the failed potential in the Hyacinth garden and the painful opposition of the whole poem between sexual discovery as intimacy and joy or as degradation and disgust. Still, "Death by Water" takes the Phlebas episode out of context, presenting only the image of a cleansing death. In "Dans le Restaurant" it appears abruptly as a release from and, possibly, consequence of revulsion at sexuality. The old waiter is told to clean himself, and the last stanza presents an ultimate purification in death. In *The Waste Land* the same passage appears immediately after the "burning" of "The Fire Sermon" and serves a parallel purpose. The shift from fire to water, from lust to a sea change, works on its own. But the story of failed desire and possibility links this movement to the narrator's memory of the garden and its replaying in "A Game of Chess."

The earlier versions of "Death by Water" point toward two kinds of experience: the horror of physical death, which becomes muted to quietness, and the release from the fires of passion. Interestingly, in the canceled first part of the manuscript version, Eliot describes sailors as somehow innocent and untouched, despite their sexual proclivities on shore, by reason of their "trade with wind and sea and snow":

The sailor, attentive to the chart or to the sheets,
A concentrated will against the tempest and the tide,
Retains, even ashore, in public bars or streets
Something inhuman, clean and dignified.[34]

It is as if the horror of life and death come from involvement in desire and decay, which the masculine world of the sea precludes. The "sea change" and the transmutation of eyes to pearls may be fulfilled in this vision of release from the world of loss and pain.

"Death by Water," as it appears in the published poem, points both backwards and forwards. It picks up images from preceding sections, and it closes off the series of poems linked by the elements of earth, air, fire, and water. Thus it allows for a new movement in "What the Thunder Said."

"Death by Water," in itself, portrays only physical death, but it carries associations from previous references to transformation and possible rebirth as well as poignant memory, failed desire, and sexual disgust. Although the conflicting attitudes of the earlier versions are foreshadowed by the fortune-teller's message of fear and the narrator's countering memory of a sea change, the latter is most evident in the strangely tranquil and silent undersea images of section 4. The implications of this section are thus complex despite its brevity. It is weighted with accumulated associations of death and new life, relief from the tensions of relationship and emotional demands, and freedom from ordinary human habitations with their city sounds, sights, smells, and crowds.

Like "The Burial of the Dead," "Death by Water" closes with an address to the reader:

Gentile or Jew
O you who turn the wheel and look to windward,
Consider Phlebas, who was once handsome and tall as you.

This time it is neither urgent nor accusing; the narrator admonishes readers to think about Phlebas, who was once like them. In "Dans le Restaurant" the description of Phlebas ends slightly differently:

"Death by Water"

"Imagine it—a terrible end for a man once so handsome and tall." The young man had been horrified by the thought of sharing experiences with an old and slovenly waiter. In this version, the narrator claims that identification for all. Phlebas, who is now drowned, was once handsome and tall, and presumably capable of desire. He must have imagined the possibility of love. Those who are now handsome and tall will share his fate and should acknowledge the significance of his death. If the narrator's first address to the reader demanded our identification with guilt, this simply calls for an acknowledgment of our human connection.

"Death by Water" provides a kind of closure to the theme of human sexuality and love. It alludes both to the repeated images of desire and loss and to the repeated hints of a transforming death by water, the "sea-change" of Ariel's song. In the end that death is not horrifying but calm and quiet, a freeing from memory and desire.

10

"What the Thunder Said"

Eliot wrote "What the Thunder Said" very quickly as a single piece. The manuscript version, unlike those of sections 1–4, has almost no cuts or revisions, and Pound's comment at the beginning is "OK from here on *I think*." According to Valerie Eliot's notes, Eliot was referring to this section in particular when he said that during certain forms of illness, "a piece of writing meditated, apparently without progress, for months or years, may suddenly take shape and word; and in this state long passages may be produced which require little or no retouch."[35] He compared such an event with mystical experience and added that you "may call it communion with the Divine, or you may call it a temporary crystallization of the mind." In this case it brought together images and dream scenes Eliot had been thinking of for several years into a single whole that is different in many ways from the previous sections of *The Waste Land*.

"The Burial of the Dead" brings together two kinds of poetic material: concrete, realistic description like the conversation with Marie or the remembered Hyacinth garden, and the symbolic, dreamlike scenes of desert rock or the Unreal City of sighing figures. Sections 2–4 consist almost entirely of the first kind. Although allusions or recurring images may link scenes with the past or with dreams of the desert or Unreal City, as in the Mr. Eugenides episode, the focus is on specific characters in realistic modern situations. In "What the Thunder Said" we have moved completely into the other realm of experience. It is surrealistic, nightmarish; the realism and immediacy of previous sections does not appear. Rather, we are in an imagined desert landscape where a figure, who is still the narrator but who now has a companion, journeys somewhere toward some unnamed goal while cities collapse and fall in the background.

"What the Thunder Said" falls outside the classification scheme of the previous sections. The four elements reappear, but none is a dominant, focusing image. What takes their place is the voice of the thunder, which comes from outside the physical world they constitute. The shift away from ordinary human life is accompanied by a shift out of the physical world into a spiritual world. The dry land, the dripping water, the wind and singing grass, lightning and the refining fire of Dante are all present, not as literal landscapes but as symbolic settings. The themes of the first part are, as the notes point out, not contemporary human relationships but the stories of Jesus, the Grail, and the postwar decay of Eastern Europe. Only the third is modern, and it is a generalized concept rather than a particular event. The theme of the second part is an Indian legend, which the narrator takes as an admonition. The section as a whole explores possible spiritual or divine answers to the "riddle of existence." This is not to say that it is Christian or even that it reaches any religious solution but only that it directs attention toward the possibility of such a solution. Yet, interestingly, the narrator interprets the thunder's answers in terms of human relationship, bringing them back into the world of ordinary experience.

Although "What the Thunder Said" may seem less immediately accessible than previous sections because it lacks realistic, dramatic scenes, it is in some ways easier to follow. It has, for the first time, a kind of plot or narrative structure in two parts. The first part is a journey across a desert that incorporates both the journey to Emmaus and the Grail quest. The "decay of Eastern Europe" is depicted as falling cities seen in the distance by the figures moving through the desert. The three "themes" Eliot notes join in this single movement. Both the disciples on the road to Emmaus and the knight on the Grail quest are moving toward some spiritual salvation that may or may not be fulfilled. In this case, nothing occurs, but the "journey" is followed by the story of the thunder, in which gods, demons, and humans ask the creator to speak. The narrator considers the meaning of the thunder's three words in his own life, and *The Waste Land* concludes in a collage of fragments reiterating the themes of the whole.

Only two voices speak in this section: the narrator and the thunder. The narrator assumes several roles—disciple of Christ, knight in quest of the Grail, modern explorer, Fisher King—and in the conclusion he recalls lines from poems and plays. More significantly, he responds to and interprets the thunder's injunctions. This is the first time that the entry of a prophetic or divine voice has elicited a positive response. In some sense, then, the narrator seems to have achieved a degree of insight, if not a solution to his problems.

The first part of "What the Thunder Said" begins in the Garden of Gethsemane, where Jesus was arrested and taken away to be crucified. The language of the first two lines links this garden directly to the Hyacinth garden: "After the torchlight red on sweaty faces / After the frosty silence in the gardens." Once again, we encounter silence in a garden, and again it refers to a betrayal of love. When Jesus went into the garden to pray, he asked the disciples to pray with him, but when he came back to them they were asleep. Twice he asked them to watch and pray with him and twice they slept and were silent. The memory of betrayed human love is transformed into a betrayal of divine love. If the potential for human sensuality as an expression of love remains as a memory throughout the first four sections and recurs as a kind of closure in "Death by Water," it is redefined here as faithfulness in a double sense. It was also in Gethsemane that Judas betrayed Jesus with a kiss and Peter denied him. His followers fail both as disciples and as human comrades.

The opening passage, then, returns to the meaning of death and rebirth in another sense, the death of Christ through betrayal, which, according to the Christian story, symbolically functions for the death of all. The restoration of Christ, like that of the pagan fertility gods, carries potential salvation for all. Both the story of Christ's crucifixion and the story of the Grail quest involve redeemers who can restore both individual and cultural life. The first passage moves from images of Christ's betrayal and agonized prayer in Gethsemane to his capture, imprisonment, questioning in the palace, and death on the cross. It is presented as violent, disturbing, hard. Color and sound and touch are all painful and intense: torchlight, agony, frosty silence, shouting, crying. Yet the final image is the thunder of spring, a hint of possible renewal. The "reverberation" of the quake that shook the earth when Jesus died merges into the sound of thunder that promises rain.

The narrator speaks for himself and another in linking his death to that of Christ. It is not clear who "we" are, but throughout this section the narrator speaks as if a companion were with him. If we take the concluding line of "Death by Water" as leading into this doubling, it may be anyone, including the reader, taken as a listener.

The following three passages depict the journey over rocky, desert land. Though the "reverberation" at Christ's death may herald rain, none yet appears. We return instead to the ruined landscape of "The Burial of the Dead" with its contrasts of sterility/vitality, dryness/wetness, rock/water, silence/thunder. The insistence on exhaustion, sterility, and longing for water are now intensified by the nightmare images of personified mountains like dead mouths and mountains filled with "mudcracked houses" and red snarling faces. The juxtaposition of a garden and rain with a rocky dead land parallels that of "The Burial of the Dead." Although Eliot did not plan this section in advance, the "crystallization" he experienced produced a kind of cyclic return to the beginning sequence.

This time, however, the scene of waste and horror gives way to a wish for a restored nature, not the nature of "breeding," "mixing," and "stirring," but a pool and a spring, with water dripping over rock and a bird's song. It is cool and quiet, without the disturbing movements of roots, lilacs, and sprouting corpses. Throughout the poem, music and the songs of birds relieve the mood of fear and terror with brief sounds of beauty. Here the hermit thrush in the pine trees evokes a moment of sweetness. The scene has a pure, inhuman quality, free of all associations with generation and decay. The passage was clearly important to Eliot. He included a long note about the purity and sweetness of the hermit thrush's song and wrote to Ford Madox Ford that "the 29 lines of the water-dripping song in the last part" were the *good* lines in *The Waste Land*." "The rest," he said, "is ephemeral."[36] Although the lines are poetically very effective, they are not so much better than the rest. It seems likely that Eliot preferred them for their content as much as their aesthetic value. They look forward to the style of his later, religious poetry, from which the anguish of sensual experience and ordinary human life is almost entirely absent. The "water-dripping song" not only contains images of moisture, coolness, and sweet song; it sounds almost like a chant, with its short lines, the strong repeated stress on "rock" and "water," and the onomatopoeia of "Drip drop drip drop drop drop drop." It is like a prayer or a dream of water. But it ends without fulfillment: "But there is no water."

The journey across the ruined land becomes, in the fourth passage, the journey to Emmaus and also an expedition in the Antarctic. What these journeys have in common is the sense of those walking that another person walks with them. In the Antarctic expedition it is a delusion, but in the journey to Emmaus it is Christ, who has risen from the tomb and is unrecognized by his disciples. Like the Hyacinth garden episode and the scene in Gethsemane, it chronicles a failure of faith or will, blindness to a living presence one longs to acknowledge but cannot. The passage itself is enigmatic; the narrator repeats that he cannot be sure of the third presence and does not know even its gender, and yet it is always there. Since Eliot's notes refer us in two directions, toward both a divine presence and an illusion, it remains imprecise and only suggestive of a redeeming presence. What happens in the biblical story is that Jesus goes into the city with his disciples. As they eat, he blesses the bread and gives it to them, and they know him. In the poem the story breaks off during the journey, at the point of uncertainty.

The theme of the "present decay of Eastern Europe" enters in the fifth passage, not as a wholly new movement but as a continuation. The desert land merges with the mountains and cities of Europe in a scene of general destruction and lamentation. London is the last in a series of cities doomed to be destroyed, and the closure on "Unreal" brings back the city of "The Burial of the Dead." Thus the narrator moves through the same desert land and city streets of the first section and sees them changed into apocalyptic visions. The dead land is hostile and the city falling. Yet the movement continues toward some possible alternative through an increasingly disturbing and surrealistic world.

The scene of the woman with long black hair and bats with baby faces was originally part of a poem depicting a journey out of a city. "So through the evening, through the violet air," written in about 1914, portrays a kind of journey into Hell and an encounter with a dead man who wishes to remain dead and forgotten. It contains a somewhat explanatory opening contrasting "words from which the sense seemed gone" with the "one essential word that frees / The inspiration that delivers and expresses / This wrinkled road which twists and winds and guesses." The image of the woman with long black hair is immediately preceded by lines that link it to the problem of lost meaning:

A chain of reasoning whereof the thread was gone

Gathered strange images through which $\left\{ \begin{matrix} I \\ \text{we} \end{matrix} \right.$ walked $\left\{ \begin{matrix} \text{alone:} \\ \text{along}^{37} \end{matrix} \right.$

The strange images were once defined as a chaos of thoughts left when reason and "the word" are lost. The choice between "I" and "we" was not made at this point, but when the lines appear in *The Waste Land*, the companion is present. This source helps define the significance of the fifth passage as part of the shift to a longing for spiritual answers to the questions posed throughout the poem. It represents the confused, disturbed world where a divine voice cannot be heard. Placed between the collapsing cities and the approach to the chapel, it intensifies the horror and strangeness of a ruined world cut off from spiritual values, not, as in previous sections, by images of death and sordid life but by nightmare visions of madness.

The journey sequence concludes with the sixth section and the "theme" of the approach to the Perilous Chapel. In the Grail legends the knight on the way to the Fisher King's castle often has a frightening adventure in a chapel or cemetery. Jessie Weston describes it as follows: "The details vary: sometimes there is a Dead Body laid on the altar; sometimes a Black Hand extinguishes the tapers; there are strange and threatening voices, and the general impression is that this is an adventure in which supernatural, and evil, forces are engaged."[38] Great importance is attached to the adventure, which the knight must survive in order to reach the Fisher King and restore the land. Weston interprets this adventure as an initiation into "the sources of physical life," which would "probably consist in a contact with the horrors of physical death."[39] The story thus has direct parallels with the story of the journey to Emmaus. Jesus has just risen from the dead, and his disciples walk with but do not immediately recognize him. His death, moreover, promises eternal life. The knight who successfully encounters the emblems of death in the chapel or cemetery may go on to restore the Fisher King and hence bring life to the land. In Eliot's scheme, it links back to and transforms the ongoing preoccupation with death and regeneration, making it part of a larger pattern of meaning.

Like the passage on the journey to Emmaus, the depiction of the Perilous Chapel is suggestive but imprecise in meaning. The narrator seems to have arrived—"There is the empty chapel"—but nothing happens and no fearful images appear. The bones, a recurring image of death and decay, are curiously freed of sinister implications: "Dry bones can harm no one." If this represents the initiation into death and sources of life, it holds little terror. Yet the passage ends in the cock's crow, which signals morning and the onset of rain. The cock may also suggest the cock that crowed when Peter denied Christ, thus linking the two stories of death and restoration.

With the chapel scene, the first part of "What the Thunder Said" closes. In one sense, it hardly seems a continuation of the first four sections, as it shifts to a symbolic landscape and presents a narrative fusing two stories of death and restoration with the "death" of modern Europe. The third theme may have been connected in Eliot's mind to the others because it first appeared as part of an early poem about a journey out from town through an eerie, surreal landscape. As a whole, the three themes become a single movement toward some religious solution to death and destruction. They form a response to the questions underlying all the scenes of death, betrayal, degraded sex, and futile lives in the earlier sections. All three represent a movement away from the horror of human life and death and toward something unclear, not yet recognized, reachable only through difficulty and courage. Although that is not defined, its associations with the resurrection of Christ and the restoration of the Fisher King imply that it is some knowledge of the way through death to new life. As each of the first four sections ended in a form of physical death and dissolution, the fifth opens with images of death as a transition to life. In the case of the Christ story, it is eternal, spiritual life; in the case of the Grail legend, it is physical renewal of the land and human life. The two are joined in the fusing of the two journeys.

The second part of "What the Thunder Said" tells another story. The legend of the Thunder comes from the *Brihadaranyaka-Upanishad,* an Indian sacred book. Groups of gods, men, and demons all ask the creator to speak. The thunder answers and says "DA" to each, but they interpret it differently as "Datta," "Dayadhvam," and "Damyata" (give, sympathize, control). The story of the thunder is a story about answering the riddle of existence. But as often happens in such stories, the answer is enigmatic and has to be interpreted, like the words of Sibyls or fortune-tellers.

In *The Waste Land* it is the narrator who interprets the thunder's injunctions, and he does so in terms of his own life. The image of rain forms a transition from the first to the second part, and the thunder's voice appears as the longed-for resolution that will release it:

> Ganga was sunken, and the limp leaves
> Waited for rain, while the black clouds
> Gathered far distant, over Himavant.

> The jungle crouched, humped in silence.
> Then spoke the thunder

Although the parts flow into one another in this way, they do not form a continuous narrative. The rain comes in a gust at the end of the chapel scene but has not yet come as the second part opens. They are linked not as a single story but as related stories pointing to the same meanings—the understanding of life and death.

Of all the divine or quasi-divine voices present in *The Waste Land,* the thunder speaks most authoritatively. Unlike the others, the thunder does not describe or comment on the human world but gives commands or what are taken for commands. The narrator responds to each by remembering a brief moment in which the command was or might have been followed.

To the command, "give," he responds with a question, "What have we given?" And he answers his own question with passionate language, as if profoundly shaken by memory:

> My friend, blood shaking my heart
> The awful daring of a moment's surrender
> Which an age of prudence can never retract
> By this, and this only, we have existed

Though the account of a moment's surrender is not specific, the very intensity of emotion it arouses grants it importance. It most easily associates itself with the moment in the Hyacinth garden when the narrator once gave flowers and called someone "the hyacinth girl," a giving of emotion that could not be sustained even immediately after. Whether that or another memory of yielding to desire, the "awful daring" takes on all life in contrast to "an age of prudence" and to the endless moments of betrayal and failure evoked by the allusion to John Webster's *The White Devil* " . . . they'll remarry / Ere the worm pierce your winding-sheet, ere the spider / Make a thin curtain for your epitaphs."

"Dayadhvam" (sympathize) elicits a somewhat different kind of response. It takes the form of three joined allusions—to Dante, the philosopher F. H. Bradley, and Shakespeare's *Coriolanus*. The first two suggest imprisonment in self and the third a momentary release from self-enclosure. The key alludes, according to the notes, to the story of Count Ugolino in Dante's *Inferno*. Imprisoned in a tower with his two sons and two grandsons, Ugolino hears the key turn in the lock. It is then thrown into a river, and the prisoners are left to starve. Eliot connects the story with Bradley's claim that for every soul the world is a closed and private sphere. "Sympathize" initially evokes thoughts of absolute loneliness and separation. The reference to Coriolanus, however, sets up an opposing possibility. Coriolanus, in a lifetime of pride and selfishness, listens and yields once to his mother, although he dies because of it. Like "give," then, "sympathize" suggests a possible surrender to others if only at great risk and only for moments.

The response to "control" is even more tenuous, a memory of what might have been. The idea of control suggests a sailboat, recalling the sailor and "you who turn the wheel." But the application to personal relationships claims only a like possibility:

> The sea was calm, your heart would have responded
> Gaily, when invited, beating obedient
> To controlling hands

The "would have" keeps such personal connection only possible and conditional.

The series of commands and responses brings the thunder's answers into the realm of personal experience and immediate human problems. With this entry of a divine voice into the poem, the concrete, physical world of the previous sections and the spiritual quest of this section come together. Whether or not he can apply them or live by them, the narrator recognizes and understands them in terms of the possibility of human contact and love. *The Waste Land* is usually seen either as a vision of Hell devoid of all spiritual values or as a prelude to Eliot's later Christian poems in which a spiritual quest is symbolically portrayed. But in this passage the two seem to join as at least one scenario among many possible ones. It does not, however, represent either the conclusion or a solution in itself, since the injunctions of the thunder run counter both to the narrator's sense of his own life and to the lives of all the characters in the poem.

The ending of *The Waste Land* is perhaps the most puzzling part of the whole. It follows the story of the thunder, but if a sense of order and understanding are there briefly sustained, they are immediately dissolved in a collocation of disconnected fragments and contradictory images. Desert, destruction, burning, violation, and madness all return, oddly combined with suggestions of hope and change.

The narrator speaks first as the voice of the Fisher King. For several reasons, the appearance of the Fisher King at the conclusion is symbolically appropriate. Although the name has sometimes been attributed to the king's devotion to fishing, Jessie Weston insists on the more profound significance of the fish as a divine life symbol, associated with Christ as well as more ancient deities connected with the origin and preservation of life. Since Eliot's notes refer us to the entire chapter on the Fisher King, he clearly meant to suggest that association. Here the Fisher King is presented with his back to the arid plain, trying to catch a fish. The image, coming after the quest scenes and the thunder's words, suggests a continuing search for the secret of restored life. But it is followed by a more modest question: "Shall I at least set my lands in order?" Juxtaposed to the fishing scene, "London Bridge is falling down falling down falling down" sets up the opposition of the entire poem between a quest for meaning and cultural collapse. Though the narrator continues to speak, and the images of fishing and of London Bridge recall earlier passages in his voice, he cannot be identified specifically with any questing figure who reaches a goal or with the Fisher King who waits for restoration. The poem does not have that consistent pattern of movement. Rather, it presents many forms of a fundamental question and poses possible answers. Both the problems and the answers remain suspended at the end.

The final lines represent what one commentator has called "a powerful recapitulation of the disorder that has been the poem's main theme."[40] The narrator's single voice breaks into fragments from many sources and in many languages:

> *Poi s'ascose nel foco che gli affina*
> *Quando fiam ceu chelidon*—O swallow swallow
> *Le Prince d'Aquitaine à la tour abolie*
> These fragments I have shored against my ruins
> Why then Ile fit you. Hieronymo's mad againe.
> Datta. Dayadhvam. Damyata.
>
> Shantih   shantih   shantih

Though these lines seem disconnected, they are linked in several ways. They reiterate themes running through the entire poem; they focus on a longing for salvation; and they make up a whole out of separate pieces in the way of Hieronymo's play. The first lines come from Dante, an anonymous Latin poem, and a sonnet by Gerard de Nerval. They translate as follows:

> Then dived he back into that fire that refines them
> When shall I be like the swallow
> The prince of Aquitaine, of the ruined tower

The first refers to the poet Arnaut Daniel, one of the souls in Dante's *Purgatorio* who are cleansed by refining fire. The second is spoken by a poet who laments that his song is unheard and longs to have a voice like the swallow. The third is spoken by a poet who refers to himself as the disinherited prince, heir to the tradition of the French troubadour poets. All three voices express a longing for purification or for the regaining of what is lost. They reinvoke, as well, earlier images of fire, the sister of Philomela who became a swallow, and the falling towers. The narrator's comment, "These fragments I have shored against my ruins," seems to imply a positive value in them, as if they provide insight or understanding by which to live, and the line about Hieronymo sustains that implication. Hieronymo, a character in

Thomas Kyd's *The Spanish Tragedy*, is driven mad by his son's murder. When asked to write a play for the court, he answers "Why then Ile fit you," and writes one made up of fragments of poetry in many languages—like this passage of *The Waste Land*. He then arranges that his son's murderers are killed in the play. Hieronymo's madness is feigned for a purpose, as this may be. Perhaps more important, the fragments chosen by the narrator are spoken by fellow poets who shared a sense of loss and a longing for some form of transformation. By articulating their memory and desire in language, they left traces that affirm the narrator's sense of the world.

Eliot's fragments end with a repetition of the thunder's injunctions, reiterating the shift from disorder and uncertainty to the only clear answers presented in the poem. Despite the emphasis on Christian themes in the journey to Emmaus and the Grail quest, their applicability or effectiveness has not been established; only the story of the thunder is completed in the form of a solution, and we do not know if it can be applied. The poem ends not in a resolution but in a kind of redefinition of the questions and possible meanings implicit in all its scenes.

The final line is like a ritual close or chant. Eliot translates it in the notes as "The Peace which passeth understanding." Although this does not really explain why it is here or how it fits in to the ambiguous ending passage, it does place the final weight on the voice of the thunder. Because it is "a formal ending to an Upanishad," it reinforces the story from the Upanishad as the nearest thing to a last word.

If we think of *The Waste Land* as the thoughts, memories, overheard conversations, and remembered quotations of a single consciousness, the closing passage reveals most directly the narrator's way of approaching and comprehending experience. What begins in private fears and dreams takes on significance and universal meaning through the recognition and appropriation of other voices, not only the contemporary voices of London society but those of all human culture. It is as if all stories, legends, poems, songs, attest to the centrality of the narrator's opening lament and the urgency of his questions. The many voices converge into the voice of one who seeks to understand the "riddle of existence" and "the doctrine for the cessation of misery," and who finds in the voices of prophecy and divine interpretation at least tentative ways of knowing. If the primary theme of the poem is that riddle, it reaches no absolute solution but only repeated assurances of some insight.

11

Allusion, Quotation, and the Mythic Method

Allusion is a reference, in literature, to another work of literature or to another art, or to history, contemporary figures, events, or the like. *The Waste Land* is so constantly allusive that it may seem almost entirely a compendium of other authors. Early reviewers often objected to this, in one case, very strongly: "Among the maggots that breed in the corruption of poetry one of the commonest is the bookworm."[41] Later readers came to see Eliot's use of other literary voices within his poetry as an important and effective technique for expanding its range of meaning and compressing many ideas and feelings into a brief line or phrase. But the function and value of so much allusion remain complex and difficult to define, especially when it takes the form of direct quotation of whole lines and passages. Does it, for example, prevent the reader from feeling a direct emotional response, as one review claimed? Does it make the poem too obscure or difficult to understand without a vast range of knowledge? More important, what is the relationship between the words of the poet and the words of the many others he quotes?

Eliot's intention in using literature as a source for his own work is partly clarified by an essay he wrote a few years before *The Waste Land*. In "Tradition and the Individual Talent" Eliot argues that poets must write with a consciousness of the past and that poetry is not the expression of personal emotion but a bringing together of new combinations of experience which may not be the poet's at all. By the first point he means that every work of art necessarily exists in relation to all the works that come before it and will come after it. For example, our sense of what makes a great play is unavoidably affected by Shakespeare, and when we see a modern tragedy like *Death of a Salesman,* we compare Willie Loman to the idea of a hero formed by Hamlet or Lear. Our very puzzlement in reading *The Waste Land* comes from expectations for poetry formed by reading the more structured work of earlier poets. For Eliot, the poet must be aware of this constant comparison and evaluation while writing. He quotes a remark that the dead writers are so remote from us because we know so much more than they and adds that they are what we know. To be modern, then, and to express what it means to be a part of one's own time, is to know and incorporate the past. Even more, according to Eliot, it is to recognize that the mind of one's country or of Europe is more important than one's own and to surrender one's own personality to it.

This surrender is his second point. Poetry, Eliot claims, is impersonal. The mind of the poet is like a catalyst; it causes otherwise disparate experience from many sources to fuse into a whole. And the more perfect the artist, he insists, the more separate will be the person who feels and the mind that creates. If we apply this theory to his own poem, the moods, emotions, and attitudes of *The Waste Land* need not originate with Eliot at all, and if they do, that is irrelevant to the meaning of the poem. What does matter is the experience evoked by the combination and arrangement of material. In the case of Eliot's dense texture of allusion and quotation from the literature of many centuries, the significant result would be the creation of a new whole of experience, complex and rich and drawing on the feelings and emotions of a long tradition of literature. "The poet's mind," according to Eliot, "is in fact a receptacle for seizing and storing up numberless feelings, phrases, images, which remain there until all the particles which can unite to form a new compound are present together."[42] *The Waste Land* forms such a new whole out of the stories, legends, images, and ideas that for Eliot form "the mind of Europe."

In discussing the development of *The Waste Land,* I have treated allusion as a means of compression by which other and wider meanings can be associated with a particular scene or image or phrase. But allusion can have other effects, as Eliot's essay makes clear. It is one way to evoke the larger, inclusive mind represented by the whole tradition of literature. Allusion, that is, may work in different directions: it may import meanings into a particular line or passage, as when the allusion to Cleopatra's barge associates the neurotic woman with both sensuality and betrayal and at the same time contrasts a past tale of passion and tragedy with a petty and passionless present. The woman takes on significance as one of many who desire and are betrayed, and yet her surroundings become cheapened by contrast. But at the same time the allusion may displace attention from the modern woman herself to a general idea of human relations as deceptive, meaningless, and futile. By generalizing experience and directing attention away from the immediate, Eliot's allusions create a commentary on society and history as well as an individual vision of the world. They are, moreover, so prevalent that many readers have taken the poem entirely as a "criticism of the contemporary world." This becomes especially true if the reader feels compelled into constant source hunting and loses connection with the rhythms and feelings of the poem itself.

Ironically, Eliot's own prose, such as "Tradition and the Individual Talent" as well as the notes, encourages such generalized and distanced readings of *The Waste Land.* By denying that the poet expresses personal emotion at all and directing attention to other literature and sources, Eliot discouraged readers from seeing the poem as a personal experience. Yet the poem includes both the voice of private feeling and the voices of tradition. To dismiss either is to limit it, as Eliot must have realized later in life when he called it personal grumbling. It is not necessary to determine whether the narrator is the poet himself in order to recognize a very specific and individual fear, loathing, and longing for change at the center of the poem. The allusion than serves to intensify and define that central consciousness and to extend its vision to a definition of the general human condition.

Allusion can function in yet another way. It involves the reader in a shared knowledge with the author. By recognizing and taking account of information outside the poem, the reader collaborates with the author in creating the meaning of a character, scene, or image. *The Waste Land* makes enormous demands on the reader's knowledge and memory or willingness to read other texts. But it also sets up a mutual understanding of shared tradition. The narrator makes this explicit when he demands that the "hypocrite reader" admit knowledge and complicity in his fear and when he speaks directly to the reader as "my friend." He insists on sharing both terror and potential salvation embodied in the meaning of other stories and the claims of other voices. If appeal to tradition in one sense depersonalizes both events and feelings, it also reduces the distance between author and reader, who share equally in that tradition.

Allusion is so fundamental a part of the technique of *The Waste Land* that it is difficult if not impossible to read the poem without some attention to sources. In many cases it does not matter either where a line came from or what it refers to in order to appreciate its effect. But in others it is difficult to see what is happening without it. For example, the opening of "The Fire Sermon" sets up a contrast between the cold, dirty, littered, and rat-infested bank of the Thames in late fall with the line "Sweet Thames, run softly, till I end my song." Without any knowledge of Spenser, one feels the opposition, and the weeping by the waters of Leman intensifies a feeling of sorrow and loss over this dying land. A recognition of *Prothalamion* and the various sources of "Leman" make the significance more precise and complex, but the feeling is evoked without it. The allusion to St. Augustine, however, is simply puzzling without the note. "To Carthage then I came" means nothing on its own, and the context will not explain it. "Burning burning burning burning" is suggestive in itself, but not necessarily of asceticism. The poem can be read, and it will have an emotional impact, on its own, but much of it would be either blank or frustrating without a recognition of the allusions. The reader must therefore consider their nature and effect and their relation to the very realistic and direct material on which they comment. It is important neither to dismiss them nor to let them displace the very real and personal emotion at the poem's center.

If allusion in itself can defer attention from the immediate situation in a poem, quotation goes further and displaces the poet's voice. Allusion need not include quotation; it may be only a suggestion in a word or a phrase such as "the change of Philomel" or "Elizabeth and Leicester," or "Prison and palace and reverberation." *The Waste Land,* however, includes many lines lifted whole out of other texts, often in other languages. The most obvious example of this is the final passage, which is almost all quotation, but many lines throughout the poem are also direct quotes or slight variations on the original. Eliot frequently uses the syntax and phrasing of a source while partially changing the words. For example, "For at my back I always hear" becomes "For at my back in a cold blast I hear." "When lovely woman stoops to folly / And finds too late that men betray" becomes "When lovely woman stoops to folly and / Paces around her room again, alone." This extensive use of quotation has several effects on the poem.

Perhaps the most striking effect is that it disrupts the narrator's voice and creates a medley of many voices. It is sometimes difficult even to tell which character is speaking, although there are usually clues in the text. In many cases quotation marks show that another voice has entered, as when the hyacinth girl or the woman of "A Game of Chess" or the Thames-daughters speak. In other cases, "I said" or "she said" distinguish the speakers, and Tiresias identifies himself. But in a few places the voice seems to change without clear signals, as when Marie takes over from the narrator in the first passage. The quotations, on the other hand, are sometimes in italics and sometimes simply embedded in the text. But if we recognize the source—and the notes usually make that unavoidable—we are always aware that another voice is present. The effect is to give the impression that there is no single continuous character in the poem. Yet the repetition of memories and images as well as a persistent set of concerns identify the recurring narrator as the same figure and the many quotations as voices of a learned tradition remembered, contemplated, and overheard. And because his mind is filled with scraps and fragments from literature, his understanding of the world is focused and defined by them. We all can think only what we have words for, and we borrow words to find expression. The narrator's voice contains and gives new expression to the many voices of the tradition of which he is a part. And the voices of the poem are both one and many as the narrator takes on many roles or finds expression through the words of others.

While quotations enlarge and enrich the range of expression available to the narrator, they also provide a way of depersonalizing his experience and emotions. Quotation removes the concerns of the poem from a private realm of suffering and grants them the greater authenticity of a general truth. Other voices continually attest to the universality of the narrator's anguish and desire. His feeling of dryness and sterility has antecedents in the Bible as God's warnings to Israel. His longing and disappointment are echoed in *Tristan und Isolde*. His weeping evokes the beauty of Spenser's Thames in an affirmation of another world. His revulsion at meaningless and crude sexuality finds authoritative expression in the words of St. Augustine and Buddha. Quotation thus provides more authentic voices to speak for the narrator and removes his unease and longing from the limitations of personal failure.

Quotation has an important aesthetic effect as well. It not only brings to bear on the theme a wider range of expression and experience, but also allows a great tonal range and flexibility. Not only his own resources of rhythm and sound are available to Eliot but all the resources of literature. An interesting example is in the opening passage of "The Fire Sermon":

> By the waters of Leman I sat down and wept . . .
> Sweet Thames, run softly till I end my song,
> Sweet Thames, run softly, for I speak not loud or long.
> But at my back in a cold blast I hear
> The rattle of the bones, and chuckle spread from ear to ear.

This is made up almost entirely of quotations from three different sources—the Bible, Spenser, and Marvell. These quotations are not exact but are very close variants that retain the rhythm and feel of the originals. The first line, from Psalms 137:1, is a lamentation with the chantlike sound of biblical phrasing. It breaks off just as the ear anticipates the kind of reiteration found in the original: "By the rivers of Babylon, there we sat down, yea, we wept, when we remembered Zion." The refrain from Spenser is melodic and gentle; it breaks the strong rhythm just begun and slows the movement by repetition and pauses in the line. The third quotation suddenly shifts to a harsh, quick movement with short words and heavy stress on consonants like *k, t,* and *b.* The swift movement from lamentation to lyric sweetness to clipped, hard sounds carries with it the feelings and themes of the sources, and allows Eliot both thematic and musical echoes. Moreover, the quotations allow for a constant modulation of sounds and rhythms that are not characteristic of modern English but are familiar to us from reading. Thus sound as well as sense expands beyond the individual and contemporary, incorporating greater possibilities of rhythm and musical effect.

The combined effect of these echoes of other authors is to reinforce and illustrate the narrator's generalization of private experience. In one sense this can be seen as quite valid. The tradition to which he appeals does offer over and over images and situations representing similar themes. The "mind of Europe" expresses itself in certain stories that share many elements. Whether Eliot as poet sacrifices his own mind to that mind and fuses into a new whole experiences not necessarily his own or whether he finds in those stories and images a mirror of his own concerns, his poem forms a continuum with them. But it is useful to remember that the tradition he calls upon is itself limited. It does not include the voices of women or the working class, and yet *The Waste Land* also speaks for them. Many of the voices introduced in the poem are those of women or the London poor, and it is questionable whether they reenact or mirror the myths of Oedipus and Tiresias or Wagner's opera or the lives of Queen Elizabeth I and her courtiers as described by historians, or that quotations from Dante, Kyd, and Verlaine represent the tradition out of which their lives are formed.

Eliot's allusions and quotations, and the notes that direct the reader toward them, set up an inclusive world in which all times are conflated and all human experience is the same, regardless of gender, class, or cultural experience. Yet at the same time the narrator is consistently present as a character limited by all these things, being male and upper-class, and living in England in the twentieth century. And although the sources on which he draws represent what has been held to be *the* tradition of Western thought, and can thus be read as making the poem a commentary on the universal human condition as it manifests itself specifically in twentieth century London, they too limit the concept of universality to the experience and thought of only part of humanity projected onto the whole. But regardless of how we evaluate the claim of inclusiveness, the use of many sources and many voices places the narrator's vision in the context of a much broader vision of humanity, one effect of which is to focus attention not on the individual but on society, and to see all lives as repeating patterns of suffering and longing for renewal.

Stories in which certain forms of experience are taken to represent universal patterns of life are called myths. One definition of myth is "a story or a complex of story elements taken as expressing, and therefore as implicitly symbolizing, certain deep-lying aspects of human and transhuman existence."[43] In his initial note to *The Waste Land* Eliot suggests that the poem is based on such a myth: "Not only the title, but the plan and a good deal of the incidental symbolism of the poem were suggested by Miss Jessie L. Weston's book on the Grail legend: *From Ritual to Romance* (Macmillan). Indeed, so deeply am I indebted, Miss Weston's book will elucidate the difficulties of the poem much better than my notes can do. . . ."[44]

Exactly how Weston's book elucidates the poem is a subject of debate. Eliot again set the direction of much interpretation by a discussion of myth in a review of Joyce's *Ulysses* written in 1923:

> In using the myth, in manipulating a continuous parallel between contemporaneity and antiquity, Mr. Joyce is pursuing a method which others must pursue after him. . . . It is simply a way of controlling, of ordering, of giving a shape and significance to the intense panorama of futility and anarchy which is contemporary history.[45]

But while the story of the Grail and references to fertility rituals appear in *The Waste Land,* they are not more prominent than references to Dante or Shakespeare, and the poem does not follow a sequence based on Weston's account. The image of a waste land runs through the whole, but that image can be found in the Bible or the story of Oedipus or the landscape of Dante's Hell. The Tarot cards, which according to Weston were first used to forecast the rising of the waters of the Nile, appear in the poem in the diminished role of fortune-telling. Two of the characters they introduce are, according to Eliot's note, associated with the Hanged God of Frazer and "quite arbitrarily" with the Fisher King. But they do not fit into a pattern of references to fertility rituals or the Grail. Aside from these images and a few brief references such as the image of fishing in "The Fire Sermon" and the line from Verlaine's *Parsifal,* the story of the Grail becomes important only in "What the Thunder Said" as one form of the journey toward salvation or renewal.

Taking *The Waste Land* on its own, without the notes, it would be difficult to say how it sustained a continuous parallel with the Grail story or fertility rituals, though present and past are constantly compared and contrasted. But if we think of the "plan" of Weston's book in a broader sense than the story it describes, I think it does become elucidative in a very significant way. Weston's purpose is to prove that the story of the Grail in its many versions is the surviving symbolic form of ancient rituals carried out to insure and sustain life and to renew the land. Her method is to insist on the single origin and harmonious relation of many, seemingly unrelated, stories and legends as a single whole. Over and over she insists on this unity in what seems to be fragmentation. At the center of all these stories, she claims, is the secret of death and rebirth; all point to that, and all the many discrete elements of the legends are ultimately parts of one overarching legend based on the cycle of the seasons. They must be studied, she insists, not as a collection of many tales but as an ensemble.

Eliot takes over only some parts of the ensemble presented in Weston: the waste land, the Fisher King, the Chapel Perilous, the Tarot, and the waiting for water. Many other elements of the story never appear. But what Eliot also follows is the notion that all these pieces are part of a single meaning. The seemingly disparate scenes and characters of *The Waste Land* are directly linked, not as part of a continuous story but as part of a larger pattern of human experience, the meaning of which is partially found in the image of a journey. The Grail story is one of several stories, along with the story of Christ and the story of a personal search for answers, that embody this pattern. Eliot's use of Weston is more a use of her method than an appropriation of the specific story she examines though the story enters into the poem.

What is most important about the Grail story itself is that it represents the development of complex spiritual symbolism out of simpler material directly aimed at physical generation and decay. Interestingly, Weston uses the words from Ariel's song about transformation in explaining the importance of the story: "If we wish to understand clearly the evolution of the Grail story we must realize that the simple Fertility Drama from which it sprung has undergone a gradual and mysterious change, which has invested it with elements at once 'rich and strange.' "[46] In *The Waste Land* as well, the images of a dead land and human isolation and sterility take on a larger symbolic value by association with images of Christ's death and resurrection, the Grail quest, and the story of the thunder. What begins in the fear and horror of individual characters is transformed into the possibility of spiritual transformation and rebirth. While this possibility becomes central only in the last section, it is foreshadowed repeatedly by the allusions to Ariel's song, "Those are pearls that were his eyes / Nothing of him that doth fade / But doth suffer a sea change / Into something rich and strange." Both Weston's and Eliot's "plans" are embodied in these lines; they express the movement from fertility ritual to the quest of the holy Grail and the movement from "April is the cruellest month" to "Shantih shantih shantih." In both cases, physical death and restoration come to symbolize a spiritual transformation, and in both a mass of seemingly disconnected incidents and images are reconciled into a unified meaning. If we read *The Waste Land* with Weston uppermost in our minds, as Eliot seems to suggest we should, we attend primarily to its symbolic implications and to the way in which all the many characters and situations, from past and present, reveal a disconnection from spiritual values and a longing for renewal. Modern humanity, in particular, appears as degraded and devoid of purpose, and the pervasive despair and fear of death are preludes to a recognition of spiritual rebirth. Tiresias, who alone in *Oedipus Tyrannus* knew the cause of the land being laid waste, speaks for all humanity in his revulsion at the reduction of the mysteries of life to casual lust.

The problem with such an interpretation is that it can easily lose sight of the specific individuality of the central consciousness. It seems clear from the manuscript version of the poem that it originated not in a broad symbolic conception but in very immediate and personal emotion. The private memories of the narrator, his sense of human loss in the Hyacinth garden, his fear of sensuality, his inability to respond emotionally, and his deep, unexplained sense of guilt are more prominent in most of the poem than the mythic pattern of death and renewal, a pattern not even carried to any resolution in the end.

The Waste Land, in fact, turns both inward toward private feeling and outward toward the human condition. The voice of the narrator sustains throughout the poem a very personal, immediate anguish and desire. But the allusions, quotations, and references to fertility rituals, Christ, and the Grail place individual emotion in the contexts of history and myth. The poem can thus be read in many layers, as a personal expression of horror at life and longing for a saving spiritual value, as a commentary on the historic human condition as always faced with human failure and in need of transformation, and as a symbolic portrayal of the modern world as a spiritual waste land waiting for the voice of a new vision. But to focus on the historic and mythic elements of the poem without acknowledgment of its personal center is, I think, to lose its strongest impact. It may be helpful at this point to return to the epigraph from Conrad that Eliot originally chose as "somewhat elucidative." *Heart of Darkness* can be read as a journey into the center of Africa, a journey back in time, and a journey within to the center of one's own soul, and there are images suggestive of all these journeys. But the ultimate discovery is Kurtz's recognition of his own soul. In like manner, the many layers of *The Waste Land* take their emotional impact and intensity from the "memory and desire" of the central consciousness.

Notes

1. I. A. Richards, *Principles of Literary Criticism* (1926), quoted in C. B. Cox and Arnold P. Hinchliffe, *T. S. Eliot: The Waste Land,* Casebook Series (London: Aurora, 1970), 51–55.

2. Jonathan Bishop, "Language in *The Waste Land,*" *Texas Studies in Literature and Language* 27, no. 2 (Summer 1985):154–77.

3. See John Paul Riquelme, "Withered Stumps of Time: Allusion, Reading, and Writing in *The Waste Land,*" *Denver Quarterly* 15 (1981):90–110; Mutlu Konuk Blasing, "*The Waste Land*: Gloss and Glossary," *Essays in Literature* 9 (1982):97–105; Margaret Dickie Uroff, "*The Waste Land*: Metatext," *Centennial Review* 24 (1980):148–66; and William Harmon, "T. S. Eliot's Raids on the Inarticulate," *PMLA* 91 (1976):450–59.

4. *The Waste Land: A Facsimile and Transcript of the Original Drafts Including the Annotations of Ezra Pound,* ed. Valerie Eliot (New York: Harcourt Brace Jovanovich, 1971), xxiii; hereafter cited as *Facsimile.*

5. Ibid., xviii.

6. Ibid., xix–xx.

7. *The Use of Poetry and the Use of Criticism* (1933; London: Faber & Faber, 1964), 144.

8. *On Poetry and Poets* (1957; New York: Noonday, 1961), 107.

9. "The Frontiers of Criticism," ibid., 121.

10. *Paris Review* (1959) quoted in Cox and Hinchliffe, 26.

11. See Hugh Kenner, "The Urban Apocalypse," *Eliot in His Time,* ed. Walton Litz (Princeton: Princeton University Press, 1973), 23–49; Grover Smith, "The Making of the Waste Land," *Mosaic* 6, no. 1 (1972):127–41; and Lyndall Gordon, "Appendix II," *Eliot's Early Years* (New York: Oxford University Press, 1977), 143–46.

12. "The Music of Poetry," *On Poetry and Poets,* 26.

13. Gordon, *Early Years,* 106.

14. Ibid., 107.

15. *Facsimile,* 148 n. 218.

16. Ibid., 2.

17. Ibid., 125 n.1.

18. Ibid., 1.

19. David Moody, "To Fill All the Desert with Inviolable Voice," *The Waste Land in Different Voices,* ed. David Moody (London: Edward Arnold, 1974), 52.

20. Ronald Bush, *T. S. Eliot: A Study in Character and Style* (New York: Oxford University Press, 1984), 64.

21. In *The Renaissance* Walter Pater described the Mona Lisa in terms that may have suggested this figure to Eliot. "She is older than the rocks among which she sits; like the vampire, she has been dead many times, and learned the secret of the grave; and had been a diver in deep seas, and keeps their fallen day about her; and trafficked for strange webs with Eastern merchants." B. C. Southam suggests this source in *A Guide to the Selected Poems of T. S. Eliot* (New York: Harcourt Brace Jovanovich, 1969), 75–76.

22. In the published poem, line 126 is "Are you alive, or not? Is there nothing in your head?" The note should be to line 125, "Those are pearls that were his eyes." Because a line was cut from the original, the numbers shifted, but the note was not corrected.

23. *Facsimile,* 126 n.5.

24. "An Unwritten Novel," *The Complete Shorter Fiction of Virginia Woolf,* ed. Susan Dick (New York: Harcourt Brace Jovanovich, 1985), 111.

25. F. R. Leavis, *New Bearings in English Poetry* (1932; Ann Arbor: Ann Arbor Paperbacks, 1960), 95.

26. Robert Langbaum, "New Modes of Characterization in *The Waste Land,*" *Eliot in His Time,* ed. A. Walton Litz (Princeton: Princeton University Press, 1973), 109.

27. *Facsimile,* 148 n. 309.

28. See Eliot's note to line 46.

29. Henry Clark Warren, *Buddhism in Translation* (1896; New York: Atheneum, 1963), 1.

30. Ibid., 352.

31. *Basic Writings of St. Augustine,* ed. Whitney J. Oates, 2 vols. (New York: Random House, 1948), 2:29.

32. *Facsimile,* 55.

33. Ibid., 123.

34. Ibid., 55.

35. "The 'Pensees' of Pascal," *Selected Essays of T. S. Eliot,* new ed. (New York: Harcourt, Brace & World, 1964), 358.

36. 4 October 1923, quoted in *Facsimile,* 129.

37. *Facsimile,* 113.

38. Jessie L. Weston, *From Ritual to Romance* (1920; New York: Doubleday, 1957), 175.

39. Ibid., 182.

40. Langbaum, in *Eliot in His Time,* 117.

41. F. L. Lucas, *New Statesman,* 3 November 1923. Quoted in Cox and Hinchliffe, *T. S. Eliot: The Waste Land,* 33.

42. "Tradition and the Individual Talent," *Selected Essays* (London: Faber & Faber, 1950), 8.

43. *Princeton Encyclopedia of Poetry and Poetics,* ed. Alex Preminger (Princeton, N. J.: Princeton University Press, 1974), 538.

44. *Facsimile,* 147.

45. Quoted in *The Waste Land: A Collection of Critical Essays,* ed. Jay Martin (Englewood Cliffs, N. J.: Prentice-Hall, 1968), 7.

46. Weston, 110.

Selected Bibliography

Primary Sources

After Strange Gods. London: Faber & Faber, 1934.

Collected Poems 1909–1962. New York: Harcourt, Brace & World, 1963.

The Complete Poems and Plays 1909–1950. New York: Harcourt, Brace & World, 1952.

For Lancelot Andrewes. London: Faber & Gwyer, 1928.

The Idea of a Christian Society. London: Faber & Faber, 1939.

Notes towards the Definition of Culture. London: Faber & Faber, 1948.

On Poetry and Poets. London: Faber & Faber, 1957.

Poems Written in Early Youth. London: Faber & Faber, 1967.

The Sacred Wood. London: Methuen, 1920.

Selected Essays. New ed. London: Faber & Faber, 1950.

To Criticize the Critic. London: Faber & Faber, 1965.

The Use of Poetry and the Use of Criticism. London: Faber & Faber, 1933.

The Waste Land: A Facsimile and Transcript of the Original Drafts Including the Annotations of Ezra Pound. Edited by Valerie Eliot. New York: Harcourt Brace Jovanovich, 1971.

Secondary Sources

Bibliography

Gallup, Donald. *T. S. Eliot: A Bibliography*. Revised and extended ed. New York: Harcourt, Brace & World, 1969. List of works by Eliot.

Selected Bibliography

Martin, Mildred. *A Half-century of Eliot Criticism*. Lewisburg: Bucknell University Press, 1972. An annotated bibliography of books and articles about Eliot from 1916 to 1965.

Biography

Ackroyd, Peter. *T. S. Eliot: A Life*. New York: Simon & Schuster, 1984. The most complete and informative biography available.

Behr, Caroline. *T. S. Eliot: A Chronology of His Life and Works*. New York: St. Martin's Press, 1983.

Gordon, Lyndall. *Eliot's Early Years*. New York: Oxford University Press, 1977. Excellent biographical study of Eliot's career through the 1920s. Includes a careful study of the history and composition of *The Waste Land*.

Critical Studies: Books

Cox, C. B., and Arnold P. Hinchliffe, eds. *T. S. Eliot: The Waste Land*. Casebook Series. Nashville: Aurora, 1970. Includes extremely useful early letters, reviews, and reactions to *The Waste Land* as well as key essays by Conrad Aiken, Edmund Wilson, Cleanth Brooks, F. O. Matthiessen, George Williamson, and Hugh Kenner.

Braybrook, Neville, ed. *T. S. Eliot: A Symposium for His Seventieth Birthday*. New York: Farrar, Straus & Cudahy, 1958. Commentaries on Eliot by many authors.

Bush, Ronald. *T. S. Eliot: A Study in Character and Style*. New York: Oxford University Press, 1983. Draws on the sources of *The Waste Land* in Eliot's private experience. It expresses his personal nightmare.

Drew, Elizabeth. *T. S. Eliot: The Design of His Poetry*. New York: Scribner's, 1949. Bases the unity of the poem in Jungian psychology.

Gardner, Helen. *The Art of T. S. Eliot*. 1949. New York: E. P. Dutton, 1959. An excellent study of *The Waste Land* as a religious quest connecting individual struggle with universal significance.

Gish, Nancy K. *Time in the Poetry of T. S. Eliot*. London: Macmillan, 1981. Two concepts of time underlie the poem: a vision of Hell outside human time and the cyclic time of the fertility rituals and Grail legends that allows rebirth.

Kenner, Hugh. *The Invisible Poet*. New York: Harcourt, Brace & World, 1959. Includes an early study of the publishing history of the text.

————, ed. *T. S. Eliot: A Collection of Critical Essays.* Twentieth Century Views. Englewood Cliffs, N. J.: Prentice-Hall, 1962.

Knoll, Robert E., ed. *Storm over The Waste Land.* Chicago: Scott, Foresman & Co., 1964. A collection of essays highlighting critical controversy over the poem.

Leavis, F. R. *New Bearings in English Poetry.* 1932. Ann Arbor Paperbacks. Ann Arbor: University of Michigan Press. 1960. An important early interpretation of *The Waste Land* as "an effort to focus an inclusive human consciousness."

Litz, A. Walton, ed. *Eliot in His Time.* Princeton: Princeton University Press, 1973. Includes excellent analyses of the original manuscript and the changes in the published text.

March, Richard, and Tambimuttu, eds. *T. S. Eliot: A Symposium.* Chicago: Regnery, 1949. Reminiscences and evaluations of Eliot by friends, colleagues, and other writers. Useful biographical information.

Martin, Jay, ed. *A Collection of Critical Essays on "The Waste Land."* Englewood Cliffs, N. J.: Prentice-Hall, 1968. A good cross section of interpretations, including key essays by Conrad Aiken and Cleanth Brooks.

Matthiessen, F. O. *The Achievement of T. S. Eliot.* 3d ed., 1935. New York: Oxford University Press, 1958. Important early study of Eliot, using his criticism to explain his poetry.

Miller, J. Hillis. *Poets of Reality.* New York: Atheneum, 1969. Includes a chapter on Eliot's philosophical sources and development.

Moody, A. D. *The Waste Land in Different Voices.* London: Edward Arnold, 1974. A collection of essays marking the fiftieth anniversary of *The Waste Land.* Valuable studies of Eliot's use of many sources and his links to music and painting.

Rajan, Balachandra. *The Overwhelming Question.* Toronto: University of Toronto Press, 1976. Considers the place of *The Waste Land* in Eliot's poetic development.

Schneider, Elizabeth. *T. S. Eliot: The Pattern in the Carpet.* Berkeley: University of California Press, 1975. Despite its beginning in many separate poems, often based in personal emotion, *The Waste Land* as published is about "a world waiting for spiritual rain in a landscape of Unity of Culture."

Smith, Grover. *T. S. Eliot's Poetry and Plays: A Study in Sources and Meaning.* Chicago: University of Chicago Press, 1956. Extremely detailed and thorough source study. Includes a chapter on *The Waste Land.*

Southam, B. C. *A Guide to the Selected Poems of T. S. Eliot.* New York: Harcourt Brace Jovanovich, 1969. Very useful set of notes to Eliot's quotations and allusions.

Tate, Allen, ed. *T. S. Eliot: The Man and His Work.* New York: Delta, 1966. Critical evaluations and reminiscences of Eliot.

Selected Bibliography

Unger, Leonard. *T. S. Eliot: Moments and Patterns*. Minneapolis: University of Minnesota Press, 1956. Useful study of Eliot's imagery.

Williamson, George. *A Reader's Guide to T. S. Eliot*. New York: Noonday Press, 1953. A helpful introduction to the poem that pays attention to its specific details of mood and image.

Critical Studies: Articles

Because so many excellent anthologies of criticism are available on *The Waste Land*, an overview of major articles up to the early 1970s can be gained by studying the casebooks, especially those by Cox and Hinchliffe, Jay Martin, and Robert Knoll. I have therefore listed only a selection of more recent articles representing new ways of reading the poem.

Bishop, Jonathan. "A Handful of Words: The Credibility of Language in *The Waste Land*." *Texas Studies in Literature and Language* 27, no. 2 (Summer 1985):154–77. *The Waste Land* is about the credibility of language. Identifies four kinds of language in the poem.

Blasing, Mutlu Konuk. "*The Waste Land*: Gloss and Glossary." *Essays in Literature* 9 (1982):97–105. The split between the poem and the notes allows Eliot to distance himself from his personal grouse.

Harmon, William. "T. S. Eliot's Raids on the Inarticulate." *PMLA* 91 (1976):450–59. A study of Eliot's ideas of speech and silence from "The Love Song of J. Alfred Prufrock" to "Four Quartets."

Lewis, Paul. "Life by Water: Characterization and Salvation in *The Waste Land*." *Mosaic* 11 (1978):81–90. "Death by Water" presents the "first of Eliot's characters who achieves spiritual renewal through an extinction of personality and an escape from time."

McGrath, F. C. "The Plan of *The Waste Land*." *Modern British Literature* 1, no. 1 (Fall 1976):22–34. A recent version of the view that *The Waste Land* takes its meaning and structure from Jessie Weston's *From Ritual to Romance*.

Riquelme, John Paul. "Withered Stumps of Time: Allusion, Reading, and Writing in 'The Waste Land.'" *Denver Quarterly* 15 (1981):90–110. Eliot's allusions evoke a relationship between poet, reader, and past poets.

Sicker, Philip. "The Belladonna: Eliot's Female Archetype in *The Waste Land*." *Twentieth Century Literature* 30, no. 4 (Winter 1984):420–31. Examines the treatment of women in the poem as central and pervasive. The archetypal female is the prostitute.

Spanos, William V. "Repetition in *The Waste Land*: A Phenomenological Destruction." *Boundary 2* 7 (1979):225–85. A quite difficult but interesting and illuminating essay arguing that *The Waste Land* is an open-ended poem rather than a closed structure. Requires some familiarity with modern philosophical terms.

Trosman, Harry. "T. S. Eliot and *The Waste Land*: Psychopathological Antecedents and Transformations." *Archives of General Psychiatry* 30 (May 1974):709–17. Analysis by a psychiatrist of *The Waste Land*'s sources in Eliot's life.

Uroff, Margaret Dickie. "*The Waste Land*: Metatext." *Centennial Review* 24 (1980):148–66. *The Waste Land* is about the play of language rather than a meaning beyond itself.

Index

Index

About the Author

Nancy K. Gish is professor of English at the University of Southern Maine in Portland, Maine, where she teaches twentieth-century British and American literature and women's studies. Her publications include *Time in the Poetry of T. S. Eliot* and *Hugh MacDiarmid: The Man and His Work*. In addition, she has held a fellowship from the National Endowment for the Humanities and written scholarly essays on Eliot, MacDiarmid, and modern poetry.